My Child, My Self
How to Raise the Child
You Always Wanted to Be

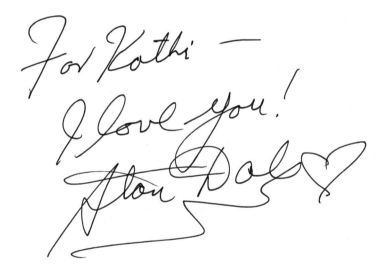

For Kathi —

I love you!

[signature]

My Child, My Self

How to Raise the Child You Always Wanted to Be

Stan Dale

HUMAN AWARENESS PUBLICATIONS
San Mateo, California 94402

My Child, My Self may be ordered from the Human Awareness Publications, 1720 S. Amphlett Boulevard, Suite 128, San Mateo, California 94402, for $8.95. See page 161 for order form.

Portions of this book not exceeding a total of 500 words may be freely quoted or reprinted without permission provided credit is given in the following form:

Library of Congress Cataloging-in-Publication Data

Stan Dale, 1929-
    My child, my self : how to raise the child you always wanted to be / Stan Dale.
    p. cm.
    ISBN 0-9631126-0-0 : $8.95
    1. Child rearing--United States. 2. Parent and child-- United States. 3. Parenting--United States. I. Title.
HQ769.D15   1992   91-35850
649'. 1--dc20   CIP

HUMAN AWARENESS PUBLICATIONS
1720 S. Amphlett Boulevard, Suite 128
San Mateo, California 94402

*This book is dedicated to
all children everywhere.
You were born a child.
No matter how old you are,
or become, you will always be a child.
Once we remember this,
we can begin rebuilding our
children, ourselves, and our planet
with dignity, love, and respect.
This is the way to end
dysfunctional families forever.*

CHILDREN LEARN
WHAT THEY LIVE WITH

If a child lives with criticism, he learns to condemn.

If a child lives with hostility, he learns to fight.

If a child lives with ridicule, he learns to be shy.

If a child lives with jealousy, he learns to feel guilty.

If a child lives with tolerance, he learns to be patient.

If a child lives with praise, he learns to appreciate.

If a child lives with fairness, he learns justice.

If a child lives with security, he learns to have faith.

If a child lives with approval, he learns to like himself.

If a child lives with acceptance and friendship, he learns to find love in the world.

Dorothy Law Nolte

Contents

A Note to You
From the Author

I wrote this book to remind us of the gods and goddesses that we all are—but have apparently forgotten. An old adage says, "If God wished to hide, he would hide in man. That is the last place man would think of looking."

If, indeed, we are "made in God's image," then we have either gotten amnesia and forgotten that, or else we believe that God is not us, but something or someone "out there." Because of that, we believe that we are more devil than god or angel. What kind of god creates pain, evil, and violence, we ask? Only gods that were taught to act and be that way. However, the good news is that what we have been taught we can unlearn or relearn.

This book is designed as a magic wand to wake us up, as well as an instrument to jar us out of that amnesia that had us forget our origins, our godhood.

Wake up, sleeping gods and goddesses! Wake up to our goodness and perfection. Wake up!

It doesn't matter how long we've been asleep. All that matters is that we are finally awake and we must never go back to sleep. We must stay diligent.

First, we must remember always that we are gods and goddesses. Who says we aren't, and why do you believe them? Next we must remember that everything and everyone we create is an expression of that perfection—that godliness. If we believe in God, God can only create perfection. If we believe in evolution—

then it has taken us about fifteen billion years to get here, and that is perfection.

We must also know that we create everything and everyone by our minds and perceptions every second we are alive. Even in our dreams.

So, this book is written as a reminder that first we must create or re-create ourselves. Then when we create our children, we can create them as we create ourselves—with goodness, godliness, kindness, and love. Then we can truly raise the child/god we always wanted to be.

The good news is there is really nothing you have to do. All that is required is to be in love. To just be! We have been human-doings for much too long. Now, it is time to be a human-*being*. . . . A being made in God's image.

So, dear reader, just see yourself as a god/goddess. See yourself as a reborn human being giving birth to other perfect beings. The more you know *that,* the more everything you do will be an expression of the goodness and perfection we were created to be.

How would you treat everyone, including yourself and your children, if you knew without a question of a doubt that you were a part of God? How do you know you are not?

From this day forward, I hope this book will assist you in knowing that. The god that is me honors the god/goddesses that is you.

I love you,

Stan Dale

Introduction

This book is about love: pure, un-adulterated, unconditional love. Love that possesses not, wants not, asks not, and manipulates not: it's love for love's sake.

Love is the highest goal to which we humans can aspire. Unfortunately, how the vast majority of people view love is really not love at all. Instead it is manipulation, violence, and possession. Most parents, I have observed, do not truly and unconditionally love their children; likewise, most children do not unconditionally love their parents. The recommendations I make in this book come from my observations of the exceptions to this rule. Because of my knowledge of these exceptions, I can say the principles I present here can and do work.

In the chapters that follow, I discuss more fully my definition and understanding of love. I also present my thoughts on the effects of our suffering from having been raised without love. I will discuss why we see so much anger, rage, disaffection, terror, and so many suicides in our culture, especially among young people.

There is a desperate search for love and meaning in our society. We repeatedly look in the wrong places and to the wrong people for answers. We look to external forces and hope someone or something will take our hand and lead us to the "Promised Land."

There is no question in my mind, we are at war with each other. Parents and their children are no exception. This book is designed to raise a white flag of truce between the combatants. Hopefully, it will become an instrument for lasting and bountiful peace. I intend to cause a revolution: a loving revolution against antiquated inhumane ideas and actions.

This book is about raising loving children. The *Random House Dictionary* defines "raise" as:

1. To move to a higher position,
2. to set upright,
3. to build or erect,
4. to promote the growth of,
5. to rear a child,
6. to activate or set in motion,
7. to present for consideration, as a question,
8. to make one's voice heard,
9. to utter a shout, cry, etc.,
10. to end a siege or a blockade,
11. to restore to life.

The tools with which to put an end to the fighting between people are within these pages. We can create a society based on dignity, respect, understanding, and trust. These are the ingredients of love. It can be done. We can replace our warlike culture with one of love.

This is not a "pie in the sky" promise. In order to participate in bringing this about, we need only to believe in ourselves and the power of love. There are very few guidelines to follow. In order to help create a society founded upon love, we simply start by bringing appreciation and love into all our interactions with everyone— including oneself. We can begin with our children and other people with whom we are very close.

When you "raise the child you always wanted to be," you can help to save *humanity through love— and in love*. Our children and other people we claim to love deserve our very best effort. It is up to us to bring love, dignity, respect, understanding, and trust into all our relationships.

The ideas contained in these pages fly in the face of tenaciously held beliefs and precepts. Within these pages is a unique concept of what is possible, support to make it happen, and a refuge for when the going gets tough. This book contains thoughts and recommended actions to breathe life into the love that has been lying dormant within us far too long.

It is time for the seed of love planted in each infant to come to fruition. There is no better place to start than at home, right here and right now, between us and our children.

1

Active
Parenting

We are such a peculiar society. We require licenses for everything from driving a car to being a beautician, mortician, or electrician. We scrutinize future employees with a fine-toothed comb. We demand references and experience for almost everything. We are even willing, at times, to train the inexperienced. We would never entrust an important job to a rank amateur. Yet, *for the most awesome, difficult, important, and necessary job of all—raising our children—little else is required of us than a short roll in the hay.*

Nine months later a child is born. Suddenly we become "parents" and are expected to have all of the expertise to match the title. As little children, we believed our parents knew everything. Now on the other side, we think we know it all. But, we don't. How can we? At best we've read a few books. We may have the example our parents set for us, much of which we probably don't want to repeat. But according to John Bradshaw, we unconsciously repeat their abuses with our own children. In becoming parents we discover the only real way to learn to be a parent is to be one. We simply try things out and discover what works.

We face an awesome task as parents: a task with little training or preparation. Many of us face parenthood with a gut-wrenching fear or an overwhelming lack of confidence. These feelings of insecurity and uneasiness lead many parents to communicate to their children, verbally and nonverbally, something to the effect of, "Look kid, don't bother me. I don't know what the h— I'm doing. I don't have any idea where to turn for help and guidance. I'm not sure I really wanted you in the first place, and I don't even know if I love you. I don't know what you need or want. Leave me alone."

The Fear of Doing It Wrong

Our fears of doing it wrong—of messing up our kids or looking bad—lead parents to do many strange and often harmful things. And yet, we don't know how or where to ask for advice. We are parents now and we're supposed to know.

If our cars break down, we generally don't hesitate to go to someone who knows about cars. We are grateful for help. If our bodies break down, we most likely go to a doctor. Why are we so reluctant to turn to an expert for help with raising our children? Why is it so hard to admit our lack of expertise?

This may be the most important step: *admitting our ignorance.* Once we have done this, there is an opportunity to learn, to experiment, to discover what truly works in raising loving children.

My intent in writing this book is to mirror, highlight, and spotlight observations, both personal and professional, that may turn on the mental light bulb known as awareness. I offer guidance and invite you to follow the beautiful path known as "active parenting."

It Ain't Easy

There are no easy answers on how to raise children. Active parenting means taking full responsibility for our actions while rearing, raising, nurturing, and loving those small and precious human beings called "children."

Active parents do not believe they have all the answers. They are willing to search, learn, and experiment. They are concerned with fostering the growth of a new human being. Active parents are involved with their children as fully and as completely as artists are with their creations. They are not intrusive, demanding, or commanding. Like the good archer described in *The Prophet* by Kahlil Gibran, they launch the arrow, in this case the child, on its way to the target. They know they cannot hold onto the arrow in its flight. Their charge is to make sure the bow and the arrow are honed to perfection through wise counsel, humanity and love. They, the archers, must prepare themselves well for this most important function in the "Game of Life."

We call ourselves world-builders, nation-shakers, generals, activists, writers, artists, revolutionaries, doctors, lawyers, psychiatrists, psychologists, teachers, or the like. We feel we are the hottest thing walking on two feet, but all for naught if we prepare our children for the world of the future in haphazard, negative, and demeaning ways. Despite all of our professional qualifications, we are all children. It is unlikely we have the necessary training to raise our children. We can all benefit by study—and by learning as we go. We can all benefit from our goal of "active parenting."

Throughout this book there are suggestions for dealing with children and other people. By applying these suggestions widely to *everyone* with whom we come in contact, we can hope to create a truly loving world.

2

The Gift of Total Permission

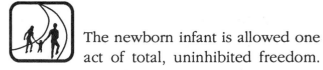 The newborn infant is allowed one act of total, uninhibited freedom. This is the last act of freedom most human beings experience.*

A baby floats blissfully for months in the perfect environment of the amniotic fluid. Suddenly its world becomes constrictive and then downright uncomfortable. Forced through the birth canal, it painfully emerges into the world of cool air, bright lights, and loud noises. Dangling upside down in space, the infant is terrified and enraged. It lets out a howl that is met with complete approval by all present.

As it cries upon entering the world, the new person is reacting to the indignities of birth. (Perhaps babies delivered by the LeBoyer Method and other water-birth methods have an easier transition.) Later, it will experience love and pleasure, curiosity and delight. The first moments, however, hold none of these emotions. Indeed, it is a near miracle that this tiny, helpless creature survives the emotional trauma of being born at all!

I wish I could tell every person on this globe never to be afraid of anything. I'd say, "You successfully lived through the strangest event of your entire life just by being born. Even though you probably cannot remember that experience, nothing you will ever encounter will be as difficult. Take heart! *You are stronger than you realize. Never be afraid.*"

* This chapter is a modification of a chapter that appeared in my first book, *Fantasies Can Set You Free*, coauthor Val Beauchamp, Millbrae, CA: Celestial Arts, 1980.

Our Downfall Begins Here

The attack on the infant's potency begins, literally, "at the breast." A newborn's most urgently felt need is for food. Unfortunately even the most willing mother cannot always respond instantly. Hence, the baby feels only its pain and powerlessness. There are other unpleasant sensations it cannot understand: heat, cold, itching, pain. . . . The baby also knows loneliness. A healthy, wide-awake baby does not like to be left alone in its crib for too long. It may cry to be picked up, fondled, and carried to a more interesting environment. Babies want intimacy.

Virtually from the moment of birth, many babies receive nonverbal messages that tell them they are not welcome and worthy human beings. Some experience tension, hostility, rough handling, or the absence of affectionate physical contact. This is all part of being an infant. The erosion of potency has been started. In most cases, this will continue for months and years to come.

There are so many possibilities for damaging a baby's beautiful, unspoiled nature. How can we, even as extremely conscientious parents, avoid them? I firmly believe we can.

It is essential that a child never be demeaned in any way, at any age. Children require a continual supply of strokes, assurance, encouragement, praise, and physical affection. A simpler word for all of this is love. Love includes dignity, respect, understanding, and trust (see Chapter 5).

It is not wise to underestimate the awareness of an infant. A human being is as aware of its feelings at the age of a few months as it is at thirty years—

often more so. Those bright eyes staring into ours perceive far more than we generally assume. It is vital that none of our messages are destructive to the baby's innate potency! The feeling of an infant's self-worth should be actively encouraged.

As conscientious parents, we are caught between what we know and how we feel. During periods of calm, we know all the right ways to handle children. We read the latest books on child care and take pride in being modern and progressive. We declare never to make the same mistakes that our mothers or fathers did with us. And yet, a father's end-of-the-day fatigue may be no match against a little boy's impudent defiance. The father may react with the same anger his own parents once turned toward him.

We parents demean children in so many thoughtless, seemingly insignificant ways. And we do this with such good intentions. We are certain our duty is to teach them to conform to family values. Seldom do we ask, or even wonder, how a child is feeling at the moment we issue an order.

Can't Violate Their Sovereignty

Often we treat children as if they are wild animals and we the tamers. They are not. *Children are as sovereign as adults.* Their value as human beings is equal to their parents'. Their small size and relative inexperience places them in an inferior position. Children are far more perceptive, aware, and capable than most of us perceive. They will naturally exhibit these characteristics if they are given permission, opportunity, and encouragement to use their abilities. Parental caution and mistrust often result in lowered self-esteem for their children.

During their early years, children are busy construct-
ing most of their beliefs and attitudes—often called
core beliefs. These patterns in their unconscious minds
will be with them for the rest of their lives. How do
we best utilize this exceptional but fleeting gift of time
in their precious first years of life? How can we plant
the seeds of self-esteem into a child's mind? How can
we instill a sense of freedom, instead of teaching fear
based on our own misapprehensions?

For example, anxious parents overprotect their children because they were taught to be afraid. Their own
fear and discomfort comes up when faced with an
unfamiliar situation. As children they were not encouraged to greet new challenges with eager anticipation
and confidence. They conceal their shaky belief in
their own abilities either by being sweet and modest
or by acting with reckless bravado. Usually, they are
unaware of the desirability and possibility of rearing
children without the limiting handicap of fear. In fact,
they believe that surrounding their children with a
blanket of caution and distrust is the best protection
they can provide.

I disagree. Inculcating fear into small children may
result in the development of unhealthy emotional
patterns. Children may learn to hold back their natural
urges to venture into new endeavors, or they may avoid
the risk of learning new skills or mastering new fields.
Children may also grow up to be indifferent and aloof.
They may hide behind a protective wall and never know
true intimacy: a tragic deprivation.

Young children always know what they want. Have
you ever seen an indecisive baby? Have you watched
a two-year-old having a hard time making a choice?
Children know and grab for whatever they want without

dilly-dallying. For some reason parents can't wait to train this remarkable ability out of them. Years later, these same children enroll in assertiveness training courses to relearn what once came effortlessly.

A typical child is born innocent and totally natural into a household of emotionally contaminated parents (themselves the product of traditional, fear-ridden upbringing). The child may express a want, only to hear, "Don't be so selfish! You can't have everything you want!" The child learns fast that whatever other people say is to be accepted as unquestionably true. The child's opinion does not matter. On the few occasions when the child gets exactly what it wants, this experience results in the child feeling good, happy, and self-assured. However, if the child persists in asking and is repeatedly refused, the often sad conclusion is to believe that the refusal is due to personal unworthiness.

Children, though emotionally perceptive, are not born all-knowing and all-wise. It takes years to acquire sufficient knowledge of the world to live safely. One of the chief functions of parents is to provide honest and accurate information. Children need time to experience and gather knowledge on their own. Permissive parents often shirk their supportive roles.

Living in Possibility

It is possible to be responsible and to give children total permission. This differs greatly from permissiveness. The permissive parent lets children do as they please. The children's actions are ignored. There is little or no support for them to be responsible for the consequences.

Permission-giving parents (as opposed to irresponsible permissiveness) also let children do as they please.

Such parents believe that children have the right to learn by taking charge of their own life. These parents give full information and are totally available should the child ask for help.

When given permission and support to be intelligent, creative, and unafraid, children are far more likely to be so. Children need encouragement to forge ahead on their own. Permission can also be called encouragement. This way of interacting tells the child or other individual, "I believe in you."

My children know my wife and I care about them very deeply. They trust and believe us when we give them permission to make mistakes. We tell them *mistakes are a part of learning, and not the horrendous evil generally supposed.* We also give them permission to actualize themselves: to tackle new projects, learn new skills, meet new and different people, and be unafraid of failing. Even if they do fail, they know that this is all right, too. They know how to extract value from experience.

By the time our youngest child was six years old, we had changed from being traditional parents to permission-giving parents. Our four boys have been responsible for their own decisions and actions. We have always given them guidance. We both want and encourage them to do what pleases them.

They have not, however, been turned loose to flounder blindly in ignorance. They have received much practical information. We have done this without using authoritarian, threatening, or restrictive methods. If it is not dangerous, each one is free to do whatever feels best. We make sure that they are aware of other alternatives as well as any hazards surrounding their choice.

Our sons know that society punishes nonconformists, even though their parents do not. We did not force them to attend school, but none dropped out. At one point one of the boys decided that school was too boring to attend. He stayed out for a week or two. When the truant officer called me, I told him that it was not my affair. I turned the astonished man over to my son. They settled the matter between them, and my son decided to return to school.

Are You a Role or a Human Being?

For years, our sons have called us "Helen" and "Stan," not "Mom" and "Dad." There is enormous sentimentality and hypocrisy built up around Mom and Dad. Two hundred years ago, European and American children were calling their fathers "Sir." This title is symbolic of the tyrannical power fathers then held over their helpless and often fearful offspring. (Many wives, for that matter, called their husbands "Sir" or "Mister.") We have come a long way since then. "Mom" and "Dad" are vast improvements over "Ma'am" and "Sir." They are still, however, tainted relics of the traditional inequity between young and old.

Formality of any sort is a barricade to intimacy—the highest, most beautiful state of human relationships. Parents are often afraid they will lose their children's respect if they allow lines of authority to break down. These parents may insist upon unquestioning obedience. They are destined for future sorrow and disappointment.

Our relationship with our sons is based on a firm, yet essentially uncomplicated, philosophy. It is this: we do not own our children. They have been entrusted to our care for the youthful period of their lives. As adults they are on their own. We are astounded that many parents treat their grownup middle-aged sons and daughters as little children. Children of any age should not be patronized or talked down to.

We have our children's respect because we respect them. Respect is a mutual affair. We consider them priceless and irreplaceable. It's like they are one-of-a-kind art objects that were put in our hands to safeguard and preserve for posterity.

In essence, we do not violate our children's sovereignty. By sovereignty, I mean that invisible psychic, emotional, mental, legal, and sometimes physical space around each human being. This is the space that belongs to each of us alone. Sovereignty is the basic right to be independent of outside intrusion. We are entitled to be autonomous in judging what is right for us to do. In simple words, our sovereignty is our total, separate individuality.

Children are children and do not usually behave as adults. Parents who are prepared to cope with each situation without feeling that the child is personally combative, are one step ahead of the game. These parents know, for example, that children sometimes break things, get dirty, tear their clothes, lose their caps and mittens, and knock over their glasses of milk. The old saw "Don't cry over spilled milk" should have a second meaning: "Don't scold your kid when he spills it!"

These parents also do their best to anticipate trouble before it becomes an emergency. They explain in quiet interludes that sharp knives can cut, fires can burn, electricity can shock, etc. They don't need to resort to fear-producing dramatics. They just explain in a way that lets the child know that the parents respect the child's intelligence. *Children are intelligent.* Their intelligence expands with each adult acknowledgment of its existence. In real emergencies, of course, parents must respond quickly and later explain the facts to the child, with love and patience.

Rearing children is not a bed of roses, even though popular fancy would have you think so. Romanticism and sentimentality surround the myth. Birth announcement cards depict angelic cherubs—innocent little lambs who have dropped from heaven to brighten our lives. They do illuminate them most of the time, but they can also infuriate.

Children are not innocent. Nobody is. Innocence is a myth: The correct word is ignorance. In a child this is not looked upon as a fault. Parents have a responsibility to fill this vacuum of ignorance with honest information. An ignorant child is a vulnerable child, unequipped for the world.* An informed child, on the other hand, is not restricted to one course of action, but has many options from which to make a personally suitable choice.

Here Is Our Humanity

Childhood is the time when the emotional patterns of life are established. It is the time for children to use and feel their emotions, including all the so-called painful ones.† They need to experience feelings of jealousy, fear, and anger. Parents should not force children to repress these natural emotions. What children do with an emotion is supremely important so that anger is not turned into violence against

* As we mature, vulnerability becomes the bedrock of potency. However, the child has not yet learned that fine-line distinction.

† See Chapter 7.

13

themselves and others. We can assist them to see the difference between rational thinking and uncontrolled rage.

We all want to surround our children with so much love that the world could never harm them. This is, of course, impossible. Parents who try to accomplish this actually do harm to their loved ones. *Children who are over-protected are like fawns raised in captivity,* then turned loose in the wilderness with no knowledge of how to survive. Allow your children to experience their lives. Let them get muddy. Let them get hurt. If they ask you to wipe off the mud and kiss the hurt place, be there for them. Give them the nurturing and guidance they need without lecturing or forcing either cleanliness or kisses! Nothing you say can compare with what they learn from their own pain. Most of all, let your children know that they are loved by you no matter what.

3

Children Belong to Life

The first and biggest mistake we parents make is assuming we own our children. We misguidedly believe our children belong to us. They do not! Children belong to life. They are not our property. They are not our chattel. The one and only thing we can truly own is our own lives. We are strictly guardians for our children until they are completely able to care for themselves. We are entrusted as custodians of the most valuable, precious entity: a child; another human life. Our children come through us. They are part of the larger picture of the universe.

It is as if the life force of the universe, seeking to perpetuate itself, devised intercourse as a fun way to do it. And "do it," we do. However, being responsible people, we must be completely accountable for our actions and the ensuing consequences. If we realize that *we don't own our children,* and allow ourselves to enjoy the privilege of watching the universe rejuvenate itself, perhaps we will treat our young differently.

When we borrow a car or some other expensive item from a friend, we often take better care of it than we do our own. If our belongings get broken or damaged, we may not like it; we may pass it off, saying to ourselves, "Oh well, I guess I didn't really want it anyway." The feeling of having our own property destroyed is nowhere near as bad as the feeling we have when we damage a borrowed item.

As a society we don't believe in owning human beings. With children, however, we act as if we believe that one little act of sex entitles us to ownership, in perpetuity, of the by-product. Old people with grown children can sometimes be seen treating their adult offspring as children. They expect them to do what they say simply because they are parents.

I do not, and will not, denigrate or point a finger at individual parents. It is not the individuals involved who are to blame. The problem lies with our programming, our system, our "scripting." I indict the whole system that perpetuates the notion that we own our children.

Be Good or I'll Kill You!

Many parents interpret ownership as implying a right to punish. How far are we willing to go with this punishment? If our children rebel, should we lock them up? If they fight back, or simply won't listen, should we hit them? How much physical force are we prepared to use? Are we willing to use a gun, a knife, a whip, handcuffs, or a jail cell? Our society encourages parents to inflict all sorts of brutality upon their children—especially juvenile delinquents.

As parents we do the best we can with the knowledge and tools available to us. Neither parents nor children are "bad people." Sometimes ignorant and confused, yes; bad, no.

At one time in my younger life, I was pretty much the kind of parent that I now decry. I was an authoritarian bully. I was narrow-minded and violent. I was trained to kill in Korea. I believed that my wife and children belonged to me. My attitude toward others was, "Don't you dare interfere, if you value your body." I didn't know better. I thought that was the way it was supposed to be. Then I began to study transactional analysis, and I learned that there was a better way, a whole new world. I got valuable input from hundreds of thousands of people on my radio talk shows and in lectures and classes. It was as if a whole new world opened up for me. *If I can change, so can others.*

I became aware that almost everything I did and said was being registered in the minds, the brains, the nervous systems of the young. My children's neuronal pathways, the linking of nerve endings of the brain, were virtually being set in concrete by my repeated actions and incantations. I discovered that whatever I say and do with my children will be with them until the day they die. All are hard-wired: the rules and regulations (good as well as bad); the rational and irrational ideas; the put-downs and insults; and the praise.

I would, as I was spanking, hitting, or yelling at them, say such moronic things as, "I am doing this for your own good. This is going to hurt me more than it will you." My children were too obedient ever to say what was on their minds. I can imagine they wanted to say, "In that case, please don't love me so much."

Our whole possessive attitude toward everything and everyone is born out of fear, anxiety, and low self-esteem. This includes our children, lovers, spouses, homes, cars, jewelry, etc.

Fear is a negative fantasy, a mental image.* Negative fantasies abound in our culture and on our planet. They outnumber positive fantasies by a thousand to one. They seem innocuous enough. They

---

* For a more complete discussion of fear, read my earlier book, *Fantasies Can Set You Free*, which I coauthored with Val Beauchamp (Celestial Arts), 1980. *Fantasies Can Set You Free* can be ordered from the Human Awareness Institute. Ordering information is in the back of this book.

sound like "Yes, but what if?" "Look out," "Be careful," "Don't do that," etc. They are overpowering and often destructive.

This Is the Garden of Eden

One way to combat these fears and insecurities is to ask ourselves, "Why would we, or anyone, want to be insecure and possessive in this Garden of Eden, where there is more than enough of everything to go around, including children?" *When we feel "not OK" about ourselves (and there aren't many of us who don't), we look for any little thing to make us feel better.* We want to believe we are worthwhile people. Every little trinket we buy is designed to make us feel better. Fancier cars, clothes, jewelry, homes, restaurants we frequent, the section of town where we live, men and women we have as friends, and the money we earn are all external attempts to make us feel better about ourselves. Does it work? Not any more than heroin. But these habits are even more difficult to shake.

Now let us bring a lover into our script: a beautiful prince or princess. Suppose we find someone who can love us in spite of the fact that we are ugly and we stink. This someone loves us, even though we may not love ourselves. There is, of course, no way we can risk letting that person go. We have to get out the whaling hooks and harpoons. We have to rope and tie them up and fence them in. We lock the gates so they may never get away. Out of fear we must own them. We claim them as ours!

To cement this sense of ownership, we get married. Then we have a baby. After the child is born, a peculiar division starts taking place. The seeds of destruction are planted. The mother devotes a lot of time and energy to the child and the father disappears. He becomes "The Phantom." Although many mothers also work, some arrange to continue to spend time at home with their children, particularly while the children are still young. Many fathers, on the other hand, make short, blustery visits to the house late in the day, only to disappear again early in the morning.

The burden on the child grows as the parents spend less time with each other due to the obligations of work and of childraising. The child becomes an important source of love and affection, as well as the glue that keeps the relationship together.

Who wants to believe we're only guardians and that eventually we will have to give up that bundle of joy? "That kid belongs to me. It's mine! That's Daddy or Mommy's little girl or boy!" If the marriage breaks up, World War III is declared to see who will own the child. Little thought is given to what the child wants or needs. The parents, judges, or social workers know best.

Children belong to themselves—and to the rest of their lives. They are human beings, sovereign unto themselves. They must not be violated. True, they are smaller than us, but their size makes them no less valuable, no less sovereign.

Kahlil Gibran stated it all so wisely in *The Prophet* when he said:

> Your children are not your children.
> They are the sons and daughters of Life's
>   longing for itself.
> They come through you but not from you,
> And though they are with you yet they
>   belong not to you.*

---

* Reprinted from *The Prophet* by Kahlil Gibran with permission of the publisher, Alfred A. Knopf, ©1923 by Kahlil Gibran; renewal, 1951 by Administrators, C.T.A. of Kahlil Gibran Estate and Mary G. Gibran.

4

Children Aren't Horses to Be Broken

People in our society have a fascination with using animal terms to refer to the actions and activities of others. Maybe it is because we are supposedly animals ourselves. We refer to many of our brethren as "bitches" and "bastards." "Men are all animals." "She's a dog." "He acts like a monkey," and on it goes. However, one expression stands out in my mind as the centerpiece of the fare we serve our children: "You can't give a kid his head or he'll run away with you." In other words, you have to keep a tight rein on "the beast" or he'll think he's free and forget who's the boss.

Before a horse can be ridden, it must be "broken." This is a totally unnatural state. However, no one can disagree that trained horses and other "beasts of burden" have made human life much more tolerable. They have been a virtual necessity since the beginning of time. At times even children have been agents of economic necessity and have had to carry their load. This is still the case in some parts of the world. Children have been used in the fields and the factories, and they did indeed work like horses. It was a matter of survival.

We Need Labor Unions for Our Children

This is the 1990s, and this is the United States. Child labor laws, for better or worse, are in effect everywhere but in the home. I am not against children working. However, I believe child labor laws must be tailored and young people allowed to work and earn their own money, as soon as possible, in the home or out. Force should not be used, of course; and certain protective factors containing provisions for age, height, weight, ability, strength, etc., should be built in. Not allowing children to work if they wish can inhibit their growth and the development of their sense of independence, and cripples their sense of self-worth. It also gives children a wholly unrealistic attitude toward money and finances.

For better or worse, we are a work-oriented society. This society is where our children will need to find their vocation. It is our responsibility to encourage them to be trained to find their place in the world of work. One of the ways we can support them is to create a realistic "work" environment for them in the home. Give them the opportunity to chose to work or not, and if they chose to do so, use this as an opportunity for learning. *Children are not,* as I fear some parents believe, *a source of free or inexpensive labor.* We must be careful not to misuse these valuable resources, the future of our planet.

As adults most of us have to work, and we do generally get paid what we are worth. The issue here is: Are our children getting their fair share? It is a rare household where the answer is yes. If we have no children, and we want to hire someone to cut the grass, rake the leaves, wash the windows, etc., how much would we be willing to pay? Surely we wouldn't expect to have it done for free. Why, then, do we expect our children to work for free? Many parents respond, "Well, I buy the kid's clothing and provide his food and shelter, don't I? And I even give him an allowance." These things are all true and they are all part of survival. We made the choice to be parents. The survival of our children is our full responsibility until they are able to provide for themselves. It is up to us to encourage them to see their value as human beings. By acknowledging them monetarily for a job well done, we help them to build healthy attitudes of self-worth.

There are many arguments in favor of the traditional attitude that children should be required to do certain things around the house. One example is "Well, I had to do it when I was a kid, and it didn't hurt me. It was even good for me." Another argument is "Things are tough, and every penny counts." True, but where is our sense of fairness? The work we did as children may have been beneficial to us, but we may be the wrong people to judge because it is usually impossible for us to see the myriad effects of everything that has been done to us or that we do to others. Many of us suffered many injustices as we were growing up. To our credit we survived. We may even have benefited from these experiences in some way. But at what price? Who knows how many things people would have done differently: how many murders, suicides, batterings, violent outbursts, headaches, ruined sex lives, and ruined marriages have occurred—all because of the abusive, unloving behavior modeled by our parents.

I do not mean to be blaming our parents and grandparents. They all did the very best they knew how. What was done is past. We can only effect change in the present. Shifting attitudes is simple, but not easy.

The first, and most important, step in raising loving children is vowing to *never raise your hand against—never to hit or spank—your child*. Never mind that you were spanked and suffer no obvious ill effects. It often takes years of experience and therapy to uncover the hidden fears and inadequacies left over from childhood. John Bradshaw in his PBS "Homecoming" series shows how childhood injuries ruin our lives.

Was Adolph Hitler a bad seed, the devil, or was he a maltreated child? Who's to say what is responsible for our troubles? What are the underlying causes of all the murders, rapes, incidences of vandalism, and other antisocial behavior running rampant throughout the world? What if they are the result of our being treated inappropriately when we were children?

My Child, My Self

I have been vilified because I say, "Treat your children as you would like to be treated." Is that really so revolutionary? Many have said it long before me: "Do unto others," "Love your neighbor as yourself," "Practice the golden rule," etc. (Notice that there never is any reference to children in these statements, no understanding that children are people, too.) The injunctions for children are: "Be seen and not heard," and "Honor thy father and mother." Shouldn't the mother and father honor the child as well, so that the children can learn how to honor and respect? I wish that all parents felt a solemn duty to be active parents and never leave their children to chance.

I have never seen permission-granting parents en masse; only in isolated cases. There are no hard facts about the practicality and results of raising children with love. There has been no documented, scientific study. What I do know is how children react to being treated with love, to being honored and respected, to being treated fairly. I have observed that these children treat their parents with equal love, honor, and respect. The same is true for adults, for each of us. Think about it: When we are treated fairly how do we respond? What makes us think that anyone else, child or adult, would respond differently?

5

Love

In my 20-year journey to find the truth about the most awesome of human phenomena—love—I have discovered some of the pieces of the puzzle. First, LOVE IS! Second, *there is really only one kind of love: Love.* Third, love and possessiveness are totally incompatible. Next, jealousy is in no way related to love. And finally, the major ingredients of love are dignity; respect; an understanding of our own and others' needs, wants, and desires; and trust.

Let us look deeper. When I say LOVE IS, I am really saying it is all around us, like the air we breathe. We only become aware we are breathing air 24 hours a day when we are deprived of it. The same goes for love. Deprive us of either for very long and we cease to exist. Tests conducted by medical and psychological researchers a number of years ago demonstrated that babies in orphanages tended to waste away and actually died if they were not held and cuddled. Children who were cuddled, touched, and held were able to prosper. Human beings apparently never lose that need, although we are experts at sublimating it.

Next, there is really only one kind of love. Suppose we say that my love for my spouse, my parents, my siblings, or pizza are all different. Aren't we really saying that my expression of love and my reactions to these people or objects may be different? *The gut level feeling, however, is the same.* I have seen many a person love their pizza with more passion and gusto than a person they say they cherish and revere.

When we're angry we can either acknowledge that fact and decide to do *nothing,* or we can strike out and injure or kill. Likewise, with love, we can acknowledge we feel love and do nothing about it, or we can spread it around, universally or selectively.

One thing is exquisitely true about love. Love cannot be wasted or hoarded. *The way to get love is to give it away.* The more we give it away, the more we get. It is self-perpetuating and regenerating. You can give away all your love and still have more than you began with!

Point three: Love cannot be possessed. This seems self-evident. However, we humans are still blind to that fact. We attempt, in every way, to possess love and those we feel can give us love. Making an effort to possess love is very much like attempting to grasp mercury. Do so, and it scatters in ever smaller pieces until there is very little, if any, left.

Jealousy, for many centuries, has been equated with love. A vast majority of us seem to believe unless our loved one says, "I love you," expresses jealousy, and indeed is willing to lay their life on the line to prove it, they don't really love us. In reality, *jealousy is the antithesis of love.* While love is, jealousy is not. There is no simple human emotion called jealousy. Instead, jealousy is a conglomerate of emotions. It is made of equal parts of low self-esteem, the fear of rejection and abandonment, anger, and a sprinkling of envy. All of these ingredients are totally toxic to love, and will kill it faster than poison will kill a rat.

The most important ingredients of love are dignity, respect, understanding, and trust. These ingredients are love's birthplace and incubator. Indeed, it is impossible to have love between two people without those ingredients. They form the nucleus for intimate, person-to-person contact.

The God in Me Knows the God in You

When we treat an individual with respect, we are respecting the god, the representative of the universe, in each of us. *Every human being has an inherent dignity.* In respecting that dignity we make it possible for love to live.

Treating each person with respect means honoring their sovereignty, their uniqueness, and their right to be self-governed. This includes children. An individual's dignity is inviolable. To be truly loving, we must deal with each individual as a representative of God.

Needs and Wants

Understanding begins with the knowledge we are all human beings whose needs, wants, and desires are fundamentally similar. We can understand another's needs, wants, and desires best when we recognize our own. Each of us has needs: things that we require, or think we require, for our survival. We also have things we would like to have. These are wants rather than needs. We often want to have them now. I am also making a distinction between wants and desires. In this analysis, desires are those things we want "someday." A desire does not have the same urgency as a want.

By understanding a person's needs, wants, and desires, we can support the person to make the distinction between these categories. We can encourage the person to obtain those things or circumstances they need or want. In interacting with children, it can be very freeing to make this distinction between needs, wants, or desires. Many children start by thinking they need a toy, or they need to do that right now. We can help them gain freedom in recognizing they may not need it, they only want or desire it.

Trust is the most crucial ingredient of love. Trust is the act of surrendering to another individual. In order to surrender to another, we must first surrender to ourselves. We must trust that we can handle whatever comes along. When we trust someone, we surrender ourselves to that person. We believe that person honors our sovereignty with respect, understanding, and love.

Even more than a statement about the other person, trust is a statement about oneself. It is only yourself you can trust. To say that you trust another is to say that you surrender to him or her, knowing that you can handle whatever the other person does.

Trust stands out by far as the single most important factor in love. Yet, it is entirely dependent upon us, not upon the person we love. Love itself resembles trust in this manner, for how can I love you if I don't appreciate and love myself? How can I really give you anything if I don't feel loved and lovable?

As a society, we are virtually bankrupt of love. We have little to give, if any. It is similar to financial wealth: A few people have the riches, while many starve. Yet we call this a land of plenty? It's no wonder the masses are much like beggars: always with their hands out, grasping for even a scrap of love.

Where did you get your personal "stash" of love? What is the quality—and amount? Did you, and do you, feel loved? How many times a day are you bathed in love's rays? Do you feel you have as much love as you can handle? Do you have any left over to give away? If you listen to the songs on the radio, read books and magazines, and watch movies, you will find a continual litany of love lost, lovelessness, elusive love, love gone astray, and unrequited love. Divorce is the norm, not the exception. Lovers, spouses, parents, children, and friends kill each other at an alarming rate. We live as if love were scarce; as if there were some finite amount available, not enough to go around.

Curing Cancer

Why is there such a shortage of love? What is this cancer of "unlovedness" that is eating away at our society? Must we continue to endure it? Is it too late for radical surgery? Is the patient terminal? I believe not. I am extremely optimistic. Whatever we humans have learned we can unlearn. *There isn't anything we can't do if we set our minds and spirits to it.*

Many cancer patients are curing their own disease by changing their attitudes and diets—or by undergoing radical surgery. It is time for our nation to do the same. We as a society need to look at changing our "diet" in more ways than one. In addition to poisoned food, air, and water, we have been fed a diet of everything our systems reject: anger, hatred, shouts, and slaps. We live with violence. Verbal and physical violence is constantly modeled on TV. We must no longer tolerate a menu of junk. As we do violence to ourselves and our loved ones, we are in effect rejecting ourselves.

To begin a new culture based on love, parents must start by unconditionally loving their children. Unconditional love is just that: love with no ifs, buts, or maybes. We can no longer say, "I love you so long as you do this and don't do that," but rather, "I love you no matter what you do, although I may not like what you do." We love the human being—*not necessarily what their programming makes them do or say.*

Children are a part of us, and the cancer of "unlovedness" is also eating away at them. We too often reject them by imposing emotional, psychological, and physical violence on them. We are so inventive. We have learned to reject them in a great variety of creative ways. We are too busy to listen to them or to spend time with them. We do not listen fully to what they have to say. We cut them off with, "That's nice, dear." We do not respect their wishes or get their vote when family decisions are made. We are just now beginning to understand the impact each little action, word, and thought has upon our youth.

Kicking the Cat

We suffer many slings and arrows in our everyday lives. To vent some of our frustrations many of us have learned to "kick the cat." Kicking the cat goes something like this: Joe gets insulted at work. He comes home and insults the first person he sees. This person, in turn, picks on the child, and the child, having no one to pick on, kicks the cat. It's time that we stop playing "kick the cat." No matter how badly we have been treated, how many injustices we've suffered, we must never, ever again "kick the cat/child."

I know there are times when each of us feels we have had it. We just can't take anymore. Sometimes we feel we can't control ourselves. We can and we must. It is essential that we change our attitudes, our "diet," get "radical surgery." It is time to take a position and do something positive.

Love! Love openly, freely, and unabashedly. Love as many people as you like, but love! Remember, the more we give to others, especially children, the more there is to go around. Love is self-renewing. It is the closest thing to perpetual motion there is. Love is indeed the only thing we get more of when we give more away.

Start now! Put this book down for a while and start giving away some love right now. Never mind feeling depleted, empty, or without love. Never mind being all alone and feeling lonely. Love is the perfect antidote. Don't worry, you really have enough love to express appreciation, no matter how down and out you feel. Start this exercise now. It's amazing how quickly it works, just like a car battery that appears to be run down. There is always that little bit left to turn over the motor; and then, like the battery, you'll begin to recharge.

If you are alone, love yourself. I mean *really* love yourself. I'm not talking about sex. Hold yourself. Touch yourself. Stroke yourself. Kiss yourself. And, as soon as you can, start spreading it around, especially to your children. If they're sleeping, wake them up. Hold them. Kiss them. Tell them that you just wanted to let them know how much you love them. Lie down with them for a while. There is nothing more comforting or loving for a child than to cuddle and fall asleep in their parent's arms. If you are with a lover or spouse, do the same with them. Remember, we are all children, and we all need love.

Let the following pages be a spotlight of truth. Let's learn to raise loving children and lovingly relate to other people. Let's overcome the old habits that have kept us at war with each other for much too long. Let those who are cynical and critical of your new actions, philosophy, and behaviors say and do what they will.

You *know* you are on the right track, and that you really do have a mission. If others say that you sound like a preacher or a zealot, fine. It's going to take an awful lot of preaching and zealousness to overcome dysfunctional life-damaging habits copied from our parents when we were children.

6

Radical Surgery

In 1972, my wife Helen, my four boys, and I performed a perfect example of what I call "radical surgery." We also "changed our diet." At the age of 42, with about $3,000 in the bank, Helen and I packed the boys, a dog, and a boa constrictor into a camper. In the following 53 weeks, we traveled 43,000 miles from the Yukon to Mexico, from Florida to Washington State, and everywhere in between.

We did not go because we were unhappy, quite the contrary. We loved our life in Chicago. I joyously worked up to twenty hours a day, slept about four hours, and bounced happily out of bed, eager to face each new day. We had many good friends. The boys were happy with their schools and friends. Helen, who was born and raised in Chicago, expressed a desire to leave, though it wasn't burning.

We left because I realized that a whole part of my life was missing. *I had always been too busy to enjoy my family.* Although we loved each other dearly, we had minimal contact. Although I was fulfilled in many ways, I wanted more time with the five people I loved most. We sold our house and furniture and bought a camper. I quit my radio job and closed my counseling practice. For the next 53 weeks, we relished the joy of being together in settings unequaled anywhere.

We traveled to many places, took in the sights, and learned a lot. Our most important lesson was how much we all loved each other. I came to know how forgiving a man's children and spouse can be. Although an accident in the fifty-third week destroyed our camper, it served to reinforce and strengthen our love for and enjoyment of each other.

Another example of "radical surgery" from my life bears retelling. It may inspire you and those you love. After twenty years in radio and about eight years before my retirement and our trip across the country, I realized that a change was necessary. Although I had a great job, it had become routine and boring. I could either take my money, shut my mouth, and continue with the status quo, or I could "change my diet."

I chose the latter. I went back to school and became a transactional analyst. As a result of my studies, I realized it was time to change the diet of crap I was feeding my children. I no longer enjoyed the role of authoritarian father. I couldn't stand the terror and pain in my children's eyes as they waited for the judge, jury, and executioner (me) to come home and address their wrongs. Loaded with my new transactional analysis (T.A.) tools, I asked my family for assistance. I told them I simply wanted to love, hold, and enjoy them. I no longer wanted to treat them worse than the family dog. I asked them to resist any harsh or unfair treatment. If they caught me acting like a bully or a dictator, they were to call me on it immediately.

A Child Shall Lead Us

Because emotions tend to run unchecked when discipline may be called for, and because I was bigger, louder and stronger than they, we devised a hand signal to act as a traffic cop for my runaway mouth. The signal, agreed upon for many reasons, was the peace sign. It had a great cathartic effect for the boys. Even though, as "Big Daddy," I gave them permission to "flip me off," they were still suspicious. They were not convinced it would work.

One day I was in the middle of giving Scott, who was about 5 or 6 years old at the time, a royal bawling-out. Suddenly, he ducked his head under his outstretched arm and gave me the signal. It stopped me like I had been struck by a bolt of lightning. In mid-sentence, I started grinning and broke into uncontrollable laughter. I grabbed Scott in my arms and hugged and kissed his frightened face until we were both laughing and crying. I held him for a long time and thanked him repeatedly. I told him how much I loved him and appreciated what he had done.

To this day I can't remember why I was so angry. It no longer matters. This was about the last time I used physical or emotional violence against my children or anyone else.

What I did wasn't magic, and it didn't work immediately. It didn't completely stop me from losing my temper, but it was a start. Like an alcoholic, I had to make an all-out commitment to my philosophy and follow through. It was a step-by-step, day-by-day process. My despised behavior changed over time, like any habit which is replaced with new behavior. For me it was a toxic habit. Now I can honestly state the habit is totally gone. I've been "clean" for over ten years.

If I, a man trained to kill in Korea, who grew up in the ghettos of New York and fought to survive in a street gang, can change, there is no question in my mind that you can, too. The question is, do you want to? Are you ready? If so, remember, take one step at a time, one day at a time, and remember to ask for help. It becomes easier with time, I assure you. And the payoff is astronomical! You can save yourself and those you love. *Each person who chooses love over violence leads us one step closer to saving the rest of the world from destruction.* For love is joy and happiness for you and your loved ones. With love and joy in your heart, there is little room for anger, meanness, and despair.

7

I Get So Mad

"I want to be loving, but I get so mad at times. I feel so angry, I'd like to choke the little bastards. They don't listen, they throw temper tantrums, they argue, they defy my every wish, and they get underfoot. It's like a duel of wits at times, and by God, I sure as h— am gonna let them know I am the boss. I am the parent and they are the children."

I don't believe there is a parent alive who at one time or another has not experienced and said either part or all of the above. That's O.K. After all, we are human, and anger is perfectly O.K. We get tired, frustrated, and worn out at times. We don't feel well. We're hungry. We have money and sex problems. All of these things happen at various times to everyone. It's times like these that strain people's souls. It's at times like these we regret ever becoming parents. We wish that we could chuck the whole thing. We're not alone in these feelings. *Remember, all feelings and all emotions are O.K. It's what we do with those feelings that may not be O.K.* What we do is entirely up to us and within our control. We can change if we choose.

Many people in our society are terrified of anger, so they stuff it until it explodes like Mount Vesuvius. *Anger is simply feeling powerless.* One way to be reminded of this is to put it in the form of an affirmation and post it in different locations at home and work. When we feel angry or frustrated (which are really all the same feeling in varying degrees), we can repeat that sentence, like a mantra. Eventually it is absorbed by the unconscious mind and becomes a natural part of our thought process. By changing our perceptions it may be possible to save our lives and the lives of the ones we love.

Anger is strictly a personal battle with ourselves. It has nothing to do with anyone else. It is a sense of powerlessness. We are not really powerless, but we *feel* that way. The adrenaline flows and our minds and bodies go into overload. Quickly reach for the circuit breaker. Reach for the "adult," the portion of our minds that resembles Mr. Spock of the TV series "Star Trek." Mr. Spock is a symbol, a metaphor, for the ultimate logical, rational, reasoning person. Everyone has a version of Mr. Spock sitting on his or her shoulder. In transactional analysis, we call this the "adult."

Each of us chooses how much of our adult we allow out at any one time. At a party or an amusement park we need very little of our adult to take care of us. At work, we may choose to let a whole lot out. A brain surgeon needs a lot of his or her adult present when operating. Can you imagine a doctor with his or her adult on a dimmer switch? Reaching into the brain, the doctor might say, "Whee! Look at the pretty little jello-y melon. I wanna play with it!" and then proceed to sink his or her fingers into the gray mass. That example may be a bit drastic, but you get the message.

If we can keep our adult on high when it is appropriate, then surely when the life and love of a loved one is at stake, we can also turn up our caring and understanding. There is no getting around it, it is one of the most difficult assignments we'll ever be asked to tackle. As they said in the popular TV program

"Mission Impossible": Should you decide to undertake this mission, the tapes will self-destruct. And the rewards will be most fruitful.

The Brain Is a River Bed

In Chapter Three I talked about neuronal pathways. Neuronal pathways are not destroyed. They simply dry up like a river bed, never to be used again. An increasingly common and popular term for these pathways is "tapes." These "tapes" are the neurons of our brain hooking up. There are about 15 billion of these neurons in our brain, a more than adequate supply. The neurons link to a "pathway" each time we repeat a thought or action. The more we repeat it, the wider or thicker the pathway becomes. Another name for the pathway is a habituated action groove. Good habits and bad habits are all equal to the brain. A habit is a habit. The pathway is very much like a fancy video tape, recording everything we see, hear, feel, taste, smell, and think. Fortunately, it is possible to record new tapes until the day we die. We are never too old to change and start new, positive habits.

The way we raise our children and relate to lovers and spouses and the things we do each and every day are habituated action grooves—tape recordings that play over and over again. We have the on/off and volume switches under our control. We are the ones who turn on the old tapes because we are used to them. They are familiar tunes. Fascinated, we listen and respond. Often, we continue to play out an undesirable tape rather than change channels. We forget there is a choice. We can choose another way to act and create a new neuronal pathway.

The No. 1 Addiction—Adrenaline

When we get angry our adrenal glands release adrenaline into our blood. Adrenaline is like "speed." It is just as addictive and destructive. Often we enjoy the rush it provides. Even when it feels lousy, it seems to feel good. I call this "perverse-delicious." "It feels so good/so bad. I'm hooked." Adrenaline makes the heart beat faster, the face turn red, the ears get hot, and the "steam" start up through the vents. We "blow our stacks," "flip our lids," "lose our cool," etc.

The reason our bodies react the way they do to adrenaline is that excess adrenaline, beyond the base level needed by the human body to keep it functioning, is toxic. What we experience is the body's attempt to rid itself of this poisonous overload. Fortunately, adrenaline burns off rapidly when one breathes long, deep breaths of air, or does some physical activity. In a short period of time the symptoms disappear.

As human beings, we experience a wide range and variety of emotions. Without them, life would be dull and flat. None of the emotions we experience are really bad. They feel that way at times because we overdose on adrenaline. My suggestion is to fully *feel* our feelings. Let the adrenaline course through our bodies. It's important to breathe deeply to avoid overdosing on the toxicity. Breathe slowly and fully; don't hyperventilate. Count to three, or twenty, or whatever is best. Pursue activity that isn't violent or directed against another person. Remember, *they* are not the problem. The battle is with ourselves. This simple formula can help us get our power back. With it, we have a good chance of winning.

Let us say that an adrenaline rush was precipitated by our young child doing something we didn't like.

How can we let a child make us do something we never would do at any other time? Why do we throw our power away? It is vitally important for each of us to stay in our power. Sure, it is possible to force a child, with brute strength and intimidation, to do something against his or her wishes. We can intimidate children, and instill fear, but, "*Is that really how we want to treat someone we love?*" Children are human beings too.

The Winning Formula

The answer to all anger is potency. A potent person rarely allows other things or people to dictate their actions. A formula I have developed describes the path to true potency: A + E = P. Awareness plus Experience equals Potency.

The more we are aware of something, and the more we do it, the easier it becomes, until it becomes second nature to us. We can actually start a new neuronal pathway and strengthen it by using the above formula. Repetition causes the old pathway to disappear and the new pathway to become automatic behavior.

As I said earlier, anger is triggered by a sense of powerlessness. No human being is ever really powerless. We can do almost anything if our attitude about it is potent. Even at gunpoint, no one can make us do something we really don't want to do. Let's say I have taken your daughter prisoner, and I have someone holding a gun to your temple. I give you a gun and tell you to kill her, or *I will*—and I'll kill you, too. You may, indeed, tell me to shoot you, because there is no way you will shoot your daughter.

I have used this analogy at hundreds of my lectures and talks. I ask women, "What would you do if I say kill your daughter or I will kill you?" Every single woman answered, "You will have to kill me." (I use daughter advisedly. We are much too willing to kill our sons in this culture.)

It is amazingly simple to become a truly loving individual. Simple, but not easy. We make it difficult by choosing the easy way, the old neuronal pathway. The challenge for those of us committed to a loving world is to learn new ways to react when angry. The challenge is to learn to allow anger, with its accompanying adrenaline rush, to pass through us without acting on it. When it has passed and we are again potent, we can choose our actions out of love.

8

Behavior

What triggers a parent's anger? What can be done to avoid the trigger? Even when we have mastered the skill of letting anger pass without acting on it, it still seems easier on our bodies and our minds to avoid the anger and the adrenaline rush in the first place.

Many parents attempt to avoid anger by imposing a host of rules and regulations on their children. Such rules are set down by individuals who think that *behavior* needs to be controlled or corrected. There is always a cause-effect relationship to all human behavior. I believe that we need to deal with the cause, not the behavior.

Behavior is what people ***do****, not who they* ***are***. Unfortunately, in our interactions with other people, more often than not what we react to is their behavior. We confuse their behavior with who they are, and when we want to support them in changing, we attempt to change the behavior rather than the cause. We punish behavior rather than taking time to find out what precipitated that behavior. The high rate of recidivism and large populations in our prisons are a perfect example of the fallacy in that kind of thinking.

Many homes are simply a microcosm of the macro-society. And unfortunately, some of them are small prisons, patrolled by guards and police who are willing to punish behavior, should one little rule or regulation be violated. Often this is done without regard for the child's individual psyche or sovereignty. It is the *law* that counts. It is the rule and the regulation that matters—not the person involved.

If we look for perfect behavior, we are looking for human robots—not individual people. Parents want everything clean and quiet. They want no mess and no noise. Children make messes, and they make noise. They create stress and strife just by being alive. They are learning to coordinate movements, and may therefore be clumsy and spill things. They need to play and get dirty. Their voices are unmodulated, so they make noise. They want what parents often cannot provide, and that creates strife. They want to do what parents don't want them to do (and they make noise), and that creates stress.

Human children are not intentionally dirty, messy creatures. It just happens that way. It's part of what it takes for a child to learn and grow. It's like the act of breathing. You can't have breath without moisture and you can't have children without noise and mess. Yet it is the rare parent who does not harangue their child to "be clean, quiet and stop being messy."

Active parents need to understand the milieu of children, so the things children need to do to live aren't a hassle for the parent. Active parents "child-proof" their home in anticipation of the child's needs. They understand the new little inquisitive creatures are not being destructive—they are simply learning. They act like good scientists. They do qualitative and quantitative analyses on everything within their reach. They pick things up and drop them, sometimes breaking them deliberately to see what happens. They learn by putting things together, taking things apart, feeling, smelling, tasting, listening, looking. They use all of their senses to make sense of everything in their world.

If adults do this, we laud that type of scientific analysis. When children do it, we get furious. Think of how many Einsteins we may have crippled in their youth because we wanted a clean home and a clean child.

The Unnatural Child

When we attempt to modify and limit children's behavior, we stifle their emotional development. We take what is inherent in the organism and warp it for the sake of peace, quiet, and order.

When a baby cries, spits up, eats, or defecates, they are just doing what they *must,* not what they want. They have no choice. It is like breathing. Stop it and you no longer have a human being. We parents are not aware that the same holds true for most of what children do. They are not perverse and destructive because of what they do. They are simply "breathing."

It is only when children are subverted, subjugated, or demeaned that they strike out in an attempt to regain their lost power. If a person is choked, they will do anything and everything to regain his or her breath. *A child who experiences being repressed lashes out, rebels, breaks the rules, etc.* Even grown-up scientists can be extremely smelly and messy. If you want an immaculate home, may I suggest you either not have children, or if you do, quickly learn to turn up your understanding, compassion, and love.

When babies cry, they are attempting to communicate with us. To most of us it is just like a foreign language. It can be grating to the nerves because we don't understand what they are saying or because they say it loudly. It's like visiting in a foreign country; if we stay long enough, and are patient, pretty soon we comprehend the language.

One mental image that has helped me tolerate a baby's cries is to think of them as similar to the sounds of whales and dolphins. I love these sounds and can listen to them for hours. We might consider crying as some not-yet-understood primordial characteristic. Our ancestors swam alongside the ancestors of those magnificent whales and dolphins, communicating with cry-like sounds. With this in mind we can begin to appreciate our baby's cries. A very short while ago that child was swimming in the amniotic seas, apparently content with its natural environment. Why be angry? The infant may not be all that happy flopping around on dry land.

We don't have to love the sounds of a crying child. Neither do we have to take our upset feelings out on the child. The same goes for anything children, or others, do to upset us. They are simply doing what they do. How *we* respond to what they do is by choice.

We often panic when a baby cries. We do not understand the language. Panic is the fear that something is wrong. It is part of our reflexive "fight or flight" reaction. Instead of reacting, listen. By listening we can quickly discover exactly what the child is attempting to convey. We find ourselves able to detect the nuances, the subtleties, the tones. Sometimes babies cry just because it is something they can do. They create and produce sounds that are uniquely theirs. Sometimes they may like to listen to the sounds of their own voices. Don't we all? To stop them from crying by doing something unnatural is like trying to shove a plug into our own mouths. *Would we want someone to do that to us?*

How we react to all of our babies' other natural functions has a profound impact on them. When a

baby spits up, defecates, or urinates, few par⌐
delighted to clean up the mess. First of all, it is he⌐
to not think of the effluvium as stinky or messy.
is, instead, the breath of life. It would benefit both
ourselves and our infants if we could learn to love its
look and smell. Well, at least to tolerate it. These
are, after all, the by-products of life. If our children
perceive we hate changing diapers, a task directly
connected with them, they may feel we hate them.
Remember, these attitudes are recorded in their neuronal pathways for the rest of our children's lives.

When it comes time to consider toilet training, don't.
I assure you, children will potty-train themselves without too much help from you. All of the coaxing, cajoling,
threatening, and rewarding, the hours spent plunking
the child down on uncomfortable potty seats or com-
mode rims are extremely destructive to the child's sense
of self-worth. The poor, confused tot may interpret
all this attention as an inadequacy on his or her part.

If we had to wash our children's diapers by hand,
it might be easier to understand the manic rush to potty-
training. In this day of disposable diapers, we can flush
away the mess without having to look at it. We powder
and perfume so it won't have to offend us.

They Die Hard

Please, please, please understand my intent and
meaning. I strive for total awareness, concern, and
love for humanity. We must all develop these attitudes
to ensure our future. We operate much of the time
from survival. We are not to blame. Our actions are
simply inappropriate. We can change, quite easily,
what we do. To change our *training* may be infinitely
more difficult. Belief systems die hard. They are the

ır upon which we stand. They are our
ns.

worry about spoiling our children. We
like food are "spoiled" by neglect, not
Spoiled children are ones who have
ᴜᴄᴇɴ ɡɪᴠᴇɴ ɪots of things and lots of so-called freedom.
They seriously lack loving understanding from their
parents. The more loving care we give our children,
the less aberrant behavior they exhibit. Children act
like spoiled brats when they are frustrated, when their
needs are not listened to or heeded.

Sometimes an individual whose needs are not being
met may exhibit model behavior. They may appear
marvelously quiet and self-contained. However, good
behavior does *not* necessarily mean good mental health.
Some of the most gruesome murders and rapes have
been performed by extremely well-behaved people,
paragons of the community.

I ask you to risk! From this moment on, take some
risks, especially where your children are concerned.
Risking is analogous to living. If you don't risk, you
may as well be dead. A plaque that I saw in a beautiful
Las Vegas gift shop said it very succinctly:

> Don't look, you might see.
> Don't listen, you might hear.
> Don't think, you might learn.
> Don't make a decision, you might be wrong.
> Don't walk, you might stumble.
> Don't run, you might fall.
> Don't live, you might die.

Live with your children, not against them. Learn
from them. Don't be so anxious to teach them the
"right" things. They will learn more about what is right
and wrong by *what* you do and the *way* you do it,
than by what you say. Learn what and who each child

is from the child—not from outside sources. Listen to your child from the very beginning.

One of the basic ingredients of love is understanding. Understand your child with all your senses. Each child is totally unique. Any similarity to any other child is strictly coincidental. Never compare one child to another. It is like comparing apples and oranges, and it can be destructive. Do not force your child into a mold, no matter what the pressures are to conform.

9

Learning

Children learn best by doing, by being involved in a process, and by using most or all of their senses. Children may not be tidy and quiet, but when they are completely engrossed in *doing,* there is no need to worry about discipline problems. When they are bored, they rebel.

There are few things more boring than being lectured to day after day. *Unfortunately, our schools have become torture chambers for our children.* They could be exciting, vibrant, and bustling places with activities suited to children's individual needs, wants and desires. Many teachers and administrators are more concerned with tidy, neat, quiet, and well-behaved robots than they are with the human beings in their charge. It does not surprise me when the "inmates" defy authority and destroy school property. They are in reaction to an archaic, inadequate system. There are many excellent, concerned, and loving teachers who are hog-tied by a system that is more concerned with money, buildings, and control than with the education of children.

Children are vibrant, vital, breathing, living creatures. They need to be stimulated or they stagnate. I want children to be animated and alive! I want them to talk, and sing, and shout when necessary. I *want* them to get dirty and experience living. I don't want my children to be good little soldiers, sitting at attention for hours and hours, afraid to stand at ease until commanded to do so. I don't want them to be lectured for hours every day. How many lectures do any of us remember? When people, especially children, are talked *to*, rather than *with*, they lose interest. Their minds turn off. I want teachers to be involved with children, talking *with* them, and learning from/with them. I want them to be treated as sovereign individuals.

Many educational reformers maintain that to deal with children as individuals requires a lot more money for education. It is criminal that our educational system is constantly constrained by lack of funds, while annual budgets for killing machines are in the hundreds of billions of dollars.

They Are Smarter Than We Think

Toddlers learn considerable skills by the time they are a year old. No one lectures them about crawling or standing up. No one makes them read books. We show them. We get involved with them. We hold their hands, hug, kiss, talk with, and encourage them. As they grow a bit older they learn nuances, idioms, and even hidden meanings. They begin to conceptualize and soon construct other concepts from their extrapolations. All this happens *before* going to school. Young children may even learn foreign languages, music, and dancing before entering a formal school.

When these junior Einsteins enter those hallowed halls, in no time flat, the innate, inborn genius starts to dissipate and disappear. They may experience themselves as a failure. How can one fail while learning? Learning may be fast or slow. Who is to say that fast is better? *A child can't fail. It is the schools that fail.* The system teaches failure.

The only time in my life I ever contemplated suicide (and that was only for a few brief moments) was when

I got my first and only "D" on my report card in grammar school. I had been ill and out of school for a week or two when my math class started to learn fractions and percentages. Until then, I had received all As and Bs. One day, totally befuddled by what was going on in my math class, I raised my hand to ask a question. The teacher, who was quite elderly and used a cane to walk and hit desks and students in anger, replied, "What's the matter with you? Are you stupid?!" Had she whispered it in my ear, it would have been injurious enough. I was sure she said it loudly enough for the principal to also hear six floors below. I was mortified. I receded within myself and never asked another question in that class.

My grades in math quickly dropped. I'm amazed that action didn't filter through to all my other courses. I felt like such a moronic failure. When report card time came, I looked at that despised symbol of stupidity and incompetence. While crossing the trolley car tracks on my way home, I contemplated letting the trolley car do me in. Obviously I didn't, but how many young people have?

There is no question in my mind that our nation and the world would be light-years ahead of where we are today if we hadn't bored our young people to death and crippled their creativity in the name of educating them.

It appears our schools abhor creativity. The more creative the child, the more they are punished. If a child expresses a creative thought, they may be put down for not coming up with the answer the teacher wanted, even if the creative answer is also applicable. There is a movement happening to change these inadequacies. More and more teachers are working to reverse this trend, and to communicate the value of the students' creative thinking. There is a move away from the lockstep and the one right answer. It is a struggling movement, fighting against decades of inertia. It is difficult to grade creativity. We can't make creativity conform to the ridiculous lockstep method we have children marching to. Instead we stunt their inherent creativity, rather than nurturing and supporting it.

Pay Attention!

When a child does or says something, I implore each of us to pay attention. Listen not only to the words, because the right words are sometimes difficult to find. Listen for the meaning behind the words. Listen to what is *not* said.

We have never really been trained to listen. We filter what we hear through our own thoughts and ideas. It is, thereby, distorted. Instead of listening, we defend, rationalize, project, and take mental excursions. We must learn to listen, to focus on the speaker as if we are experiencing an intricate work of art.

Communication is a complex art. Sometimes children don't believe their parents listen to them. Unfortunately, this is often true. Most parents have the same complaint. Children learn by example. *Most parents lecture rather than talk with and listen. Shut up and listen! You might learn something.*

It serves no purpose to provide remedies for each unwanted behavior. I could fill a book that way, and it would be of no real benefit to anyone. When we approach a child with love, an open mind, and a willingness to listen and learn, we can do little wrong.

All the right things to do are of no avail without the right attitude. Any child or aware adult can see through and reject a phony front. Instead of making any real difference, we perpetuate the cancer that is never treated. Band-aid measures only drag out this fatal cancer of humanity. Radical surgery is mandatory. We can pussyfoot around the issue all we want, but I guarantee you, we are playing with the lives of all present and future generations.

Radical surgery is really what this book is all about, though it makes a rotten title. As I've said many times before (and I will continue to repeat), the best and only form of radical surgery is love, dignity, respect, understanding, and trust.

As with food, love can't be shoved down people's throats. All we can do is what we do, the way we do it. Everything we do must come from a love for self, and for all of humanity. Anything and everything else is a rip-off. As parents we can take responsibility to have what we do and say be something we are proud to let the world, and our children, see and hear. Remember, our children learn from our actions. We are their primary role models. If we do things that are hypocritical, we shouldn't be surprised when our children follow our example. It is as simple as "do unto others."

This does not mean we must suddenly be perfect. We often do and say things without thinking. There are many things we wish we could take back or wish we had never said or done. That's O.K. It's never too late to reevaluate what we've done. We can ask our loved ones to forgive the "old" us who did or said it that way. We can promise that the "new" us chooses to be different. By doing this we show our humanity. We admit that we are not infallible.

This means we don't try to stay on a pedestal. When we admit we've done something undesirable that we would like to correct, the child realizes they can admit they're not perfect, too. The child learns by example to go back and correct mistakes. They learn to be flexible in their ability to change and grow. It's amazing how long we hold onto things that do not serve us, even when we don't want to. By getting off our position, we give ourselves and our children permission to let go and create new and better ways of looking at old thoughts and ideas.

Talk with your children about their perceptions of your behavior. Ask for their input. You will be amazed how much you will learn. You will show your children that you are willing to become more aware and concerned. Children are amazingly perceptive individuals. If they see that you are making an attempt to change, they may gladly meet you more than halfway. Enlist your child as a helpmate, friend, buddy, and confidant. Pretty soon you will have your child as an ally instead of an enemy. And allies almost always act in our, as well as their own, best interests.

10

*Children
in Loving
Families*

A loving family works together for common goals. Children are included in a way that makes their contribution clear and their feelings valued. Cooperation becomes a natural way of living, and the rewards for the young people include a wealth of possibilities. *Children who are nurtured in loving family settings need never fear being alone or being put down or left out.* They have many people to love who love them. These are people who will nurture, teach, and advise them, and with whom they can share and confide their deepest thoughts and feelings.

In this environment, they need never harbor deep, dark secrets because they know they will never be rejected, no matter what they may do, think, or feel. When tasks need doing, they are asked, never ordered, to participate and to contribute to the family. Children love to imitate their parents, no matter what they're doing, when they feel they have a choice not to and won't be demeaned and/or punished.

Punishment is a dead-end street. When we punish a child, how far are we willing to go? Are we willing to hit? If the hitting doesn't work, what then? How much force are we willing to mobilize against our own flesh and blood? Three to five children die per day at the hands of their parents and at least a million others suffer such severe physical harm that they have to be called to the attention of the authorities. *How far are we willing to go?*

When we punish our children, we teach them negative things. We teach them, when all else fails, to use violence. Is that what we really want to teach our children? Behavior modification may change the behavior, but at what expense? Always it obscures the *causes* of that behavior.

Slavery Is Outlawed Except for Children

When various chores around the house present themselves, ask yourself first, "If I didn't have a child, who would I get to do it? Would I do it myself?" Who will wash the dishes seems to be one of the bigger problems facing most families, even if they have a dishwasher. Parents are torn between teaching the children the "right" things to do, and the feeling that they are being ripped off by insensitive, uncaring children. *Don't wash the child's dishes for him or her!* Stop rescuing your children, period. The more you treat your children like cripples, the more they will indeed become "crippled."

So many parents believe they are showing love for their children by taking care of all the necessities of life for them. They are loath to stop that type of destructive behavior. For many mothers, it is a way to feel useful and loved. They *do* things for their family, so their family will love them. This is such a mistaken notion. We don't have to *do* anything to be loved. We need only be who we are.

In teaching children to do the despised dishes, you may start by doing your own, and maybe a pot or a pan. Use no more than if you were cooking for yourself alone. Put all unused dishes away. Soon the children will realize that in order to have clean dishes for the next meal they'll need to wash a dish or two. The same thing goes for making beds, taking out garbage, and the like. Use your human creativity. The results can be astounding. When this kind of creativity is applied even-handedly from the very beginning, it becomes as totally natural as everything else in the child's environment.

Parents can do the dishes with the little child a time or two, showing concern and love. Then as soon as possible, wean themselves away from the child's task. Nurturing, active parents seldom breed resentment and rebellion in their children because they do not act as hypocritical plantation owners who used slaves to do their dirty work.

Any attempt to make the child take responsibility must take into account the child's age and ability level. Even a young child, say four or five years old, can bring their own dishes to the sink to be washed, even if they are not yet old enough to wash them. Similarly, young children can keep their toys in their own room and do many things for themselves. Creative, active parents can facilitate this by designing the environment and tasks to support a child's sense of responsibility. This is well worth the short-term work for the parent.

To have a truly cooperative house, we cannot behave like dictators. It is our duty and responsibility to provide our children with a home. If each child is fortunate enough to have their own room, fantastic! If not, creative minds working together can usually solve most problems. *Privacy is extremely important for every human being,* especially maturing children. A simple little device like a separate tent for each child, even in the same room, can work wonders.

We need not order our children to clean up their rooms to communicate the importance of being responsible for things. If indeed, it is "their room," give them total responsibility. Don't butt into their privacy. However, if the children repeatedly mess up some other part of the house with their stuff, for example the family and living rooms, and entreaties don't work for whatever the reason, one option is to dump those things into the trash. It doesn't take children very long to discover that if they want to keep their things, they can't just leave them anywhere. Of course, do not replace the discarded items or buy new and different ones.

The *children have to learn that all freedoms have responsibilities.* There is no need to be punitive. It is important to treat children in the same way we do anyone else who deposits a mess in our living room.

What I am saying is, stop taking away children's responsibility. Rescue is not an act of kindness or love.

Radio and TV commentator Paul Harvey relates a story about his dog, whom he loved so much that his daily acts of love and kindness eventually killed it. Paul would bring out a sweet treat for his dog every time his dog did something Paul liked. Pretty soon the dog became addicted to the sweets, got diabetes, and died. How many destructive and detrimental things we do to our children (and each other) in the name of love!

Let us take a moment to examine at some length a few other things that have become everyday, routine actions and functions.

Mealtimes

Most families have some mealtimes together. I contend that establishing these times may be one of the most oppressive things we do in the name of love. Mealtimes seldom take into consideration the individual's own body-clock. Everyone is forced into a lockstep method of operation where the individual's needs and wants succumb to those of the family.

A person may not be hungry at the prescribed mealtime or feel like eating the dishes prepared. Yet we must stop what we are doing, no matter how interesting, enjoyable, and important, and join the family for a meal. If we don't show up and eat, we may feel we are sabotaging family harmony and unity. We risk personally offending the cook, who may have worked long and hard preparing a masterpiece. *Preparing food is one of the insidious ways "mothers" have of receiving strokes and praise.*

Most of us have our prepared meals *when* we want them and how we want them. The subtlety of the oppression is that one person usually has the job for life. Who cooks for the cook? I know many women proclaim they really love to cook, and they get great joy out of watching their families appreciate their efforts. If cooking is one of the only sources of compliments and strokes a person receives in an average day, it may be difficult to relinquish this stroke-producing activity. Additionally, mealtimes, especially dinner, may be the only times the family gets together. It's a wonder that even greater emphasis isn't placed on mealtimes.

I want to clarify that I am not against family mealtimes. They can be great fun, and times for much joy and companionship. What I am against is the pressure to conform that often surrounds them. Family members, especially the children, feel they have few (if any) options. Mothers are put in a similar bind. They, too, feel there are few options, except the occasional night out, when they go to a restaurant or dine at a friend's home.

If a person is a good cook, and *really* enjoys preparing a meal, great! However, don't assume that cooking the family's meals is that person's job for life or that everyone always wants to eat the food prepared. Don't presume everyone will attend a preset mealtime. Allow freedom for someone to eat a hot dog instead. Let them be responsible to prepare it. If someone doesn't want to eat, don't badger them. Just accept that as his or her wish, and say, "Great." If the family wants to eat together, or take food to their rooms, or eat only one meal a day, why not? What is your personal involvement and investment in their preferences?

In many subtle ways, we feel compelled to do things we don't necessarily find desirable. This is one of the greatest destroyers of personal potency and self-esteem, and one of the most insidious forms of oppression.

Many men report that they feel like human cash registers for their families, and not much else. *It is difficult to go to bed with a cash register.* Conversely, women complain they feel like a "three-legged cat in a sandbox," or a "doormat," or both. What have we evolved into, and when is this going to stop?

Coming to the Fair—Play

In truly cooperative households, there are many options and alternatives. Workloads inside and outside of the home can be divided so no one is stuck doing anything unpleasant for long periods of time. With this kind of an arrangement, wives and husbands can get strokes from more than housework or outside work, and not feel trapped in either one.

As a family unit, sit down as soon as possible and use all of your creativity and brainpower to decide on ways that everyone (not just some) will be able to get most of their needs met, most of the time. Be sure you are all honest. Don't try to protect anyone's feelings. This is harmful to the person being protected and is not likely to yield the best possible solution.

Do one or two people set the rules for your family, or is it done cooperatively and collectively, without the rule or the ruler becoming oppressive? The rule must never be more important than the people involved.

Children need to be allowed and encouraged to make meals for themselves and others—if they wish. Preferably they should do this at the earliest age possible. Provide the necessary information, then let the children make their own choices. Let them know as much as possible about nutrition, the benefits of a balanced diet, and the dangers of too much sugar or fat. You can limit the types of food available to your family, but remember they may go elsewhere to get what they want. The best way to encourage your children to eat well is to do it yourself. Even if they experiment with other foods, they are likely to appreciate your example in the long run.

Never lecture children about food preparation. Teach them that following a recipe is an art. Help them to create their own ways of preparing food. As long as you don't have to eat it, let the children experiment.

Schools

I don't believe children should be forced to attend school. They should be encouraged to get an education, but public and/or private schools may not be the best source. One of the greatest forms of oppression and repression may be the compulsory education laws of the state. Parents are obliged to have their children attend school under penalty of law. This is due to the constitutional right for each child to have an education. Some states are allowing parents to set up and send their children to a wide variety of in-home and alternative schools. Not all forms of alternative education have been successful. At least an attempt is being made to discover forms of education more suited to individual children's needs.

When we were on our year-long trip, the living, daily, out-of-class education received by our children almost made them misfits when they first arrived at their new Santa Rosa schools. They were so turned on, and imbued with so much knowledge, they caused minor disruptions for the schools involved. They were accustomed to active hands-on learning. The adjustment to sitting at a desk in a classroom was not easy.

On the trip, each little thing they saw or experienced became a teaching device and learning tool. We didn't have to send out for films about the out-of-doors. We learned everything we could together firsthand. Highway signs were English lessons and even lessons in Spanish and French when we visited Mexico and French Canada. They learned arithmetic from the trip meter and speedometer in the car. Later they all became good drivers. They learned about money and home economics by using their own money to buy what they needed. We had books galore but didn't force them to read. We gave them many opportunities, at the earliest possible ages, to experience driving the car in safe, off-highway areas.

Many of our sons' new-found acquaintances in Santa Rosa were extremely envious. In the beginning, this created a great deal of difficulty. Eventually they all voiced how lucky they felt the Dales were. They wished they could have a similar experience.

Children should have total responsibility for anything and everything concerning school. This includes responsibility to get up and get ready: to setting their own alarms (and turning them off); to preparing meals, washing, and dressing; to getting to and from school (including arranging public or private forms of transportation); to studying; to doing homework; and to deciding what time to go to sleep. The child can learn to manage his or her life dealing with these situations. This impresses upon the child from the beginning that an education is their responsibility and not his or her parents'. That is a hard-won victory. A marvelous side benefit is that it also makes the harried job of being a parent that much easier.

When my wife and I decided to become active parents, we bought each boy his own alarm clock. The first ones were gifts from us, but any replacement was their own responsibility. We continually impressed upon them that they were responsible for their own lives. If one of the boys overslept, he was responsible for the consequences as an adult is for being late for work. The same was true if he didn't want to go to school. We had fully discussed the consequences of each action with them, including the fact that *we,* as parents, were required by the school administrators to account for their actions.

To this day, our sons have done nothing to necessitate our reporting or explaining their actions to the front office. We allowed our children the opportunity to take "mental health days" off from school when they felt the need. We felt this to be better than concocting lies about their absence. These were their personal holidays. It still amazes me how few they took. It also amazes me how early they set and kept their own bedtimes. If I had been given the same opportunity, I probably would have stayed up to the wee hours just to prove I could. They never did.

Transportation

If one of them wanted "wheels," that, too, was their business. When asked by any of our sons, we discussed the options and alternatives we knew. Then he was on his own to look for, buy, finance, and maintain his own car. By age sixteen, each of our boys had his own means of transportation. One of the boys had eyes larger than his means. He spent years paying for his impetuous decision. He could not have received a less expensive college-type education. What he has learned from all of the ramifications of this experience, however painful, is invaluable. The rest of the family members (myself included) are grateful for our ancillary learning experiences.

Sibling Rivalries

If there are sibling debates or actions, do not intervene. It is not your problem. Let them work it out and *refuse* to step in between, no matter how they beg and plead. So-called sibling rivalries seldom raise their ugly heads in cooperative family settings. Where there is no scarcity of love or loving resources, children do not need to compete for love.

If, however, the children ask if you are *willing* to mediate, be sure they understand you are acting only as a mediator and that this is not an everyday occurrence. Make it clear that the people in the relationship have the task of working out the difficulties. Your job is to offer some new thoughts and perspectives that may have been clouded over by the combatants' emotions. As parents, you may not be the ideally suited person for that particular mediation. Another family member, even an outsider or a paid professional, may be better suited. The reasons and dynamics may be varied and complex. In any event, each situation must be handled in the most adult way.

Labor/Management = Children/Parents

Here are a few simple rules to make mediation more effective:

1. Make sure all of the parties involved "cool off" for a mutually agreed-upon period of time. A walk or some time in private will suffice.
2. During this cooling-off time, they are to ask themselves what they could have done differently and what their part was in the flare-up. How are they responsible?
3. When the cooling-off period is over, all parties sit facing each other, as if attempting to settle a union/management contract dispute.
4. Writing instruments are provided so notes may be taken.
5. The "no response rule" is strictly adhered to. This means each person has an opportunity to speak without interruption until they are complete. When the next party takes a turn, no response is allowed to anything the other speaker(s) said. Sometimes more than one round of no response is required.
6. A dialogue is begun only after each person has had an opportunity to speak. The mediator makes sure each person sticks to the issues involved and doesn't go off on tangents by bringing in past history and irrelevancies.

7. The mediator is an intermediary or referee. A mediator does not meddle or take sides and attempt to provide solutions to the problem. If a solution is offered, be sure it is offered as a *possible* solution, and not the *right* one. The people involved need to come up with their own unique solutions.

8. Finally (and if all else fails), in certain unique situations "binding arbitration" may be necessary. That is, if the aggrieved parties fail to come up with a solution, they agree to abide by the decision of the mediator. This is only to be used very sparingly, and with great reluctance.

Treat all participants as intelligent and creative people. The basic problem is that their "lenses" are clouded over and their perception is veiled. The mediator's role helps them "clean their lenses" so that they can "see the light."

Far fewer divorces and breakups would occur if adults were to use these techniques. *Children learn best by example.* If they see their elders handling problems in adult ways, they are very likely to follow suit. That is also why many parents are considered hypocrites by their children. Parents continually *tell* their children what to do and what not to do. Meanwhile they themselves do the very things they supposedly decry. Your children will learn far more from your actions than your words. Don't be surprised when your children mimic your behavior as they grow older.

No family or grouping of people will ever create a Utopia. When people relate to each other or live together, there is a geometric progression of problems. That is, problems tend to multiply in direct proportion to the number of people involved. Two people have one relationship, three people between them have three relationships, four people have six relationships, five people have ten relationships, and so on. However, as problems multiply, so can joy and happiness.

If the basic philosophy of the group/family is to treat each other with dignity, respect, understanding, and trust, and to be a cooperative unit rather than a competitive one, most difficulties can be overcome. This may not be an overnight miracle. Nor should we expect no strife and unhappiness to occur with everyone living "happily ever after." It doesn't work that way. Nonetheless, it has to be better than our normal way of operating.

We can make the changes necessary to have cooperative families work. There is little we humans can't do, once we take the challenge.

Unity within diversity is the main result of raising a family from a foundation of cooperation and personal responsibility. I look forward to this in the future—for our nation and the entire world. As we do it in our families, then I believe the society at large will also benefit enormously. We all win when one's individuality is preserved in the family or the group and when the well-being of the group or family is not subverted by the individual. If we dream the so-called "impossible dream," who knows what's possible!

11

Self-Esteem

Self-esteem is the hard-won bedrock on which life's foundations must be built. The fresh confidence and optimism that was ours at birth and in our early childhood days is too often eroded by the time we are in our teens.

Children begin life in a state of self-delight, experiencing everything in their immediate world as wonderful. Gradually, and sometimes all too quickly, these little beings learn that they are not O.K. To be accepted by parents, siblings, teachers, and peers, they learn to do things and act in unnatural ways that may be unacceptable to their emerging sense of self. This requirement to conform, to behave unnaturally, sets up an unconscious conflict about what is right, natural or expected. As this happens, they develop an internal push and shove between the unconscious mind that generates their emotions and the conscious mind that creates their thoughts. They're divided against themselves. They're split—no longer whole.

Children are taught to get along by suppressing their own inward rhythms, feelings, and perceptions in favor of those of their caretakers. Yet, who are *they?* Who *are* those paragons who serve as models for their lives? Are they not products of the self-same pattern? Were they also encouraged to sell their souls?

Self-esteem may be the single most important factor in determining an individual's sense of well-being and subsequent behavior. If I feel like a victim with little or no self-esteem, there is a great probability that I will think of myself as "a worm," "a snake," "a rat," "a skunk," or "a pile of trash," and act accordingly. Conversely, doesn't it stand to reason that if I feel like a king or queen, a prince or princess, or see myself as an eagle flying high and free, or feel like a million dollars, then my chances of self-actualization, of feeling and acting as a magnificent human being, are greater.

It is ultra-important that we do not demean ourselves, our children, or anyone. We cannot be phony and say things we don't mean. Children usually feel or intuit the truth behind our phony facade. They have a remarkable ability to remember off-hand remarks. Unfortunately, they sometimes lack the sophistication to know how we intended them. Everything we say can make a long-lasting impression. Therefore, it's important to be aware of what we say and do at all times. We must be like careful, concerned gardeners especially when our children are in their formative years. We must carefully and tenderly nurture this young being, or it will grow crooked and bent, if it grows at all.

Self-esteem is the way we perceive ourselves. It is how we relate to ourselves and our environment. It's the *realistic* picture of the way we see others and the way others see us. It's the high and favorable regard in which we hold ourselves, when those around us cast stones of derision.

As We Think, So We Are

Our ancestors, in an attempt to make us humble and non-egotistical (a tactic designed to preserve the sovereignty of the state/church), planted seeds of self-doubt and destruction. When we doubt ourselves, we buy into what other doubters think and say. Only doubters (people with low self-esteem) cast aspersions upon others. It's like the game of "hot potato." A hot potato is tossed to me, so I have to toss it to someone else as fast as possible or be stuck with it when the buzzer sounds. The person holding the hot potato is the loser. In life, not wanting to appear the loser, we throw critical feelings to anyone who will take them. Unfortunately, we are such willing creatures, we stand, arms outstretched, ready to catch them.

The next time someone attempts to throw you a hot potato, don't take it—no matter what form it's in. Avoid the negative beliefs of others at all costs. If you are called something nasty or rude, don't believe it. Why get angry when lies are being told about you? Observe the other person's actions and words when they throw you their not O.K. feelings. They are simply attempting to make themselves feel better. That's why so much prejudice exists in our society. It's an attempt to make the holder of the prejudice feel better. It's supposed to put one a step up from another person. After all, if someone is beneath us, we are not at the bottom of the heap.

When someone calls me something unpleasant, I may reply, "Oh, something about me bothers you. Do you want to talk about what that is and why it bothers you?" It is obviously not me the person is talking about. I know I am not what they called me. They were attempting to throw me their hot potato. By not grabbing it, I don't play the game. I decline to perpetuate feelings of not O.K.

I don't spend much time worrying someone might be right in their evaluation of me. I *know* who I am. I realize they must not feel their own perfection to cast aspersions on someone else.

How can human beings be anything *but* perfection? Isn't it interesting we continually say, "No one is perfect"?

It's strange that you never hear those same people say, "Stars and oceans aren't perfect."

Everything in the stars is in us, and everything in us is in the stars. We are one with the stars and the universe. *The universe is perfect and we, as a part of that universe, are perfect.* If we believe in a God, or a creator, we must believe in perfection. Can perfection create anything but perfection? If the belief in a God eludes us, and we instead believe in evolution, then our evolutionary status at this precise moment in history is exactly as it is supposed to be, and that is perfection. To think of ourselves as *anything but perfect* is to demean not only ourselves, but all of creation, evolution, and the universe.

Unfortunately, many people believe that "perfection" thinking is counterproductive. They believe that to think they are perfect is to limit themselves and their potential. The reasoning goes something like this: "If I am perfect, I need never do anything to improve myself. I am already there." Then they use this to say that if they are perfect there is no reason to change anything.

True, we are already perfect. But *perfection is not stagnation.* A star, perfect though it may be, is always changing, always evolving. A star goes through many phases, yet always it shines. When we know our own perfection, then we shine like stars, too. A star can't think deep, dark thoughts and turn itself off. Only we human beings can. We have control over the degree to which we shine.

I'm O.K.—You're O.K.

Perfection is the realization that all others are also perfect. It is truly the realization that "I'm O.K.—You're

O.K." When we feel O.K., we experien
esteem. When we experience high self
hold others in high esteem and treat them

Other people are mirrors of what we feel
If I see you as horrible, I really see myself in your
reflection. If I see you as a loser, or a victim, or not
O.K., I really see that reflection of myself—a reflection
I don't like. The saying "We hate most in others what
we hate most in ourselves" is an absolute truism. Turn
it around, and that saying is also right on the mark:
"What we love in others is what we most love and strive
for in ourselves."

As parents, one of our most important functions is
to reaffirm our children's inherent sense of O.K.-ness.
We must ensure that everything we do and say is based
on the firm conviction that what we are and do is
perfection. The smallest demeaning remark or action
can erode another's sense of self-worth. One seed of
negativity can do a lot of damage, particularly with our
children.

From the beginning, we must say and do things
with our children (and others we love) that continually
reaffirm: "I believe in you. You are O.K. You are
perfection. You are wanted. Nothing you can do can
make me not love you. If you do something I don't
like, it will in no way reduce my love and affection
for you." We must also do this for ourselves. We must
know that because we are human, we may lack
awareness and experience in many areas. What we
do may not be perfect, but who we *are* is always perfect.

Unfortunately, the odds appear to be overwhelm-
ingly against growing up with a strong sense of self-
esteem. Feelings of inferiority, low self-esteem, victimization, and powerlessness abound.

As a society, we destroy much of the natural perfection of our planet. We pollute our air, food, and water. We destroy our forests and oceans. We level mountains and trees so we can have more asphalt and concrete. It is no surprise that we do the same thing to ourselves. We take what is natural and beautiful about ourselves and make it appear to be not O.K.—even ugly.

That beautiful, shining star of our self that was our birthright is overshadowed by ignorance and fear. We must do everything possible to reverse the trend before it is too late. We must wage an all-out war against everything that erodes our self-esteem. We must make the acquisition and maintenance of self-esteem our highest priority in life, and especially in the rearing of our children.

12

All This Mess in the Name of Love

One of the difficulties we encounter is our own conditioning. We have been taught all our lives to act in ways that protect us from phantoms and to assume the world in which we live is unloving. As a result, much of what we automatically do and say, despite our best intentions, works against our efforts to love. This is often unconscious, and considerable effort is required to bring us to awareness.

Each day, we communicate in innumerable ways our lack of trust and lack of faith in ourselves and others. These horrendous attitudes and behaviors had to originate somewhere. They are unnatural. They do not begin at birth. They are learned. As the song in the musical "South Pacific" says,

> You've got to be taught to hate and fear.
> You've got to be taught from year to year.
> It's got to be drummed in your dear little ear.
> You've got to be carefully taught.

And we are taught, from the cradle, to hate, fear, and protect ourselves and our loved ones. This protection shows up in many ways, not the least of which is lying. In the larger society, lies appear to be the norm. Everyone lies. Relationships are not as they appear. Advertising gives us hype about a product—and experience tells us the truth. Not to lie is to feel like a "Stranger in a Strange Land."

A Lie Is a Lie

There are two basic types of lies: overt lies and covert lies. The overt or bald-faced lie covers every arena from the unabashed intentional lie to those "little white lies" we pretend don't mean anything. Overt lies are the ones we speak or do. The covert lie is never verbalized. It is "lying by omission." What needs to be said is left unsaid.

Most of us would be amazed to find out how many times we knowingly and unknowingly lie. We think we must lie to get others to do what we want. So much so, that if we stopped and counted the number of times we lie in an average day, we would be shocked, amazed, and dumbfounded. Do it some time, and remember that overt, covert, and "little white lies" are all the same. We lie to ourselves and others because we are afraid to tell the truth, afraid the other person (and we ourselves) won't be able to take it.

To put on a false face and act in ways we don't really feel is lying. Lies are insidious because we may not truly be aware of what we do or say. The person with the perpetual grin or smile may be lying. We must break through the shroud of ignorance and fear. Hopefully ever-increasing numbers of us will penetrate this shroud in the future.

A lie is primarily a protective device. Lies are told because the teller believes that the listener can not, and will not, be able to handle the truth. In reality, it is the teller who is unable to handle his or her prediction of the listener's response. The expected response precipitates the lie in the first place. It is intended as a way to protect each other. The price is awesome. Lies keep both teller and listener victims. They never learn to handle stressful situations with honesty.

Nothing destroys trust more quickly than to lie to those we love. Trust is one of the most important cornerstones of love. When we lie to our loved ones, we produce a lie, not a relationship. When we lie, we aid in the victimization and crippling of those we say we love. We don't allow them to take personal responsibility for their actions. We say, in effect, that the person we lie to is too weak and too stupid to handle what we've already handled. We think we are being loving when we lie, but what we really do is prevent *ourselves* from feeling the possible pain of dealing with the other person's actions and emotions.

Many relationships and marriages collapse because they are built on lies from the beginning. A loving relationship cannot be built on lies. To do so is to guarantee that everything connected with the relationship will tumble down one day, as if built on quicksand.

Often we think less of ourselves and others for lying. When we recognize a lie to be a protective device, we need not demean the person telling it. If the person had a high level of self-esteem, there would be no need to lie.

Thus people with high self-esteem feel no need to lie. They *know* they are O.K. and need not fear. They stand firm on the bedrock of high self-esteem with the reins of their life firmly in hand. They are neither egotistical nor narcissistic, because they know that people who exhibit that behavior are *not* feeling O.K. but are attempting to put on a brave front. High self-esteemers feel secure in their actions and thoughts and know there is little, if anything, they can't handle. And they extend the same dignity, respect, understanding, and trust to everyone else they meet.

Fear of the reaction of others cause many people to act in ways diametrically opposed to their true feelings.

For loving relationships without lies, we must learn to tell the truth and ask for what we want. We must also learn to listen to what is *really* going on behind the false face or act, and support our children and other loved ones to be honest.

Jealousy—The Green-Eyed Monster

What does jealousy have to do with love? We say, "I am jealous because of how much I love you." I don't believe it. Jealousy, that crippler and destroyer of relationships, is bred in the swamps of low self-esteem. It can never grow in the strong sunlight of truth and honesty. It festers and oozes, taking over healthy, loving people's lives, and deposits them on the trash heaps of humanity.

Eighty-five percent of all murders in our society are "crimes of passion," and one of the most common reasons is "jealousy." *Jealousy is a conglomerate of low self-esteem, anger (feeling powerless), fear of rejection, fear of abandonment, envy, and a sprinkling of other negative trace elements.*

A person with high self-esteem who experiences jealousy recognizes that jealous feelings are a warning about something they may want to change in themselves. An aware person knows they don't necessarily have to *do* anything about such feelings, and they definitely don't have to respond by throwing a temper tantrum. In addition, they realize that to act out or act on those feelings may cause pain or damage to someone else or themselves.

We are brought up to believe that love cannot exist without jealousy (and vice versa). I categorically disagree. I am certain that jealousy and love are incompatible. Jealousy is no more an expression of love than is violence. Jealousy is a survival instinct. Although it may have been bred into us when we were living in caves, there is no discernible evidence to deem it a necessary or important habit to cultivate within ourselves or others.

Discipline

Another potentially damaging act in the name of love is to discipline our children. There is one simple question that, with the powerful force of a machete, will cut down the underbrush that traps us in our past and clouds our senses when it comes to raising loving children: *"Do you allow yourself to be treated that way?"*

Do you allow yourself to be hit or spanked? Do you want someone to scream at you? Do you want to be left to cry alone when hurt, locked in your room, or stood in the corner? Imagine being sent to bed without food and in so many ways treated like a dangerous criminal and prisoner. Do you permit anyone to shove food down your throat whether you like it or not, and then be threatened with all sorts of punishment if you don't act gratefully, as if you enjoy it? Do you like being *ordered* to clean your room, take the garbage out, wash the dishes and the car, and take care of your brothers and sisters? Do you allow someone to tell you what time to be home and go to sleep whether you're sleepy or not, all the time feeling they don't trust you?

The list is endless. Each and every one of these (and all the ones not mentioned) demean, destroy, degrade, and vilify both parent and child. Yet all of them are done in the name of love, because we care about our children and somehow think this type of treatment helps them grow up to be better people.

There is never any reason to spank or hit a child, or anyone else! When we hit children, we teach them many things. They learn how not to love or respect us, and to use violence to make others do what they want.

Nothing raises the hackles of "good people" quicker than to see a bully pick on a smaller guy. We are even horrified when a larger animal attacks a smaller one. Yet we allow a 200-pound person to pound on a 2- or 3-foot tall, 30-to-40-pound girl or boy. We condone this as being a good parent!

Hogwash! Insanity! Why, in the name of humanity, do we allow this to continue? The major answers, of course, are ignorance, fear, anger, and frustration. The use of the word ignorance is not intended as a put-down. Ignorance means that someone is: "lacking in information or lacking in knowledge and training; uninformed or unaware."

Many parents fear their children will not "turn out right." They fear they will become criminals, bums, or sex maniacs. They go on the offensive almost from the moment a child comes out of the birth canal. If our children don't turn out the way we wanted them to, we consider *ourselves* failures, and we lash out in anger and frustration. In addition, as parents we are often conscious that our parents, relatives, neighbors, and friends are watching. Sometimes it seems they are all waiting to yell out, "If you were a better parent, your child wouldn't have turned out so poorly. I knew you'd fail!"

Our society now exhibits all kinds of unloving behaviors. We do not need to perpetuate this way of living. In the name of love we can eliminate hate, lies, jealousy, and cruel discipline. We can start with our own lives and with what we teach our children. That's what it's all about.

13

Honesty and Asking for What You Want

Little babies are completely honest. It is natural for them to put out for what they want, and to keep asking until they get it. They don't worry about what anyone else thinks of them, or whether they look bad. They don't worry about anything. They just ask. They only stop asking for what they want when we, their parents, and others in society, tell them it's not O.K.

We do this because of our own feelings that it is not O.K. to ask. This feeling was taught to us by parents, who learned it from their parents, who learned it from their parents. In fact, almost everyone in this society is afraid to ask for what they want or to be honest. We fear that others will think poorly of us or respond adversely to our requests.

We have been brought up to believe that to ask for what we want is self-centered, egotistical, or worse. In our dealings with others, we are led to believe if we have to ask, it's not worth it (whatever *it* is). Everything is supposed to happen as if by magic. Therefore, we have learned not to ask. We put on a humble face, and pretend we don't want whatever it is we truly desire.

Almost from birth, we are taught never to ask for what we want. We hear "don't" or "shouldn't" all the time. "Don't do that." "Don't ask for this." "You really don't want that." After all, what will other people think?

"Never ask for or do what you want, and never be honest," is drummed into our heads day after eternal day. According to our "teachers" it is better, for some unknown reason, to deny that we need or want anything. These lessons are based primarily on what other people might think or say. What a horrible way we have been taught to live!

The first place to effect change is in our home with each member of the family—little step by little step. Every positive move forward helps obliterate the negative programming. Encourage your children (as well as everyone else you love and care about) to cooperate with you in making these changes. Support is invaluable as you embark upon this new venture. It's new territory for you. You'll feel shaky at first. There are no absolute rules, and very few, if any, guideposts on this journey to self-fulfillment.

Ask, It's Good for You

As children, before we learned that asking was a "no-no," we asked all the time. Our children do the same. It's as natural as breathing. Sadly, most of us have been "choked" quiet. When we do begin to ask, we feel marvelously exhilarated. It's as if we have removed an oppressive strangling hand—and are finally able to breathe freely and be our true selves.

When we were mere babies, we asked for milk. We asked in our infant way and we asked until we got what we wanted. We didn't have to raise our hands and ask, "May I?" If we wanted to crawl or walk, our parents were delighted to let us, at least for a while. It was all right to become potent and powerful, but only to a point. Our parents' programming caused them to question and limit our behavior. It's as if they were saying, "What and who do you think you are?" and "What will other people think?"

By asking for what we want of ourselves and others—100 percent of the time—we embark on becoming fulfilled, actualized people. This positive new habit can supplant and supersede all the old toxic garbage we have learned. Eventually, new habits become ingrained in our neuronal pathways. The more we practice, the easier this becomes.

It makes infinitely good sense to ask for 100 percent of what we want, 100 percent of the time. Even though we don't always get the full 100 percent, we have a far greater chance to come close to our wants by asking. If we don't ask, it is likely we will receive nothing at all.

If you learn to ask for 100 percent of what you want, 100 percent of the time, be willing to hear "no." When you begin to negotiate the rest, you will increasingly notice positive results. This is so very simple, but oh, so difficult to do. Many of us don't know what we want. Knowing our wants was trained out of us when we were small children. If we *do* know what we want, we often don't know how to get it. The antidote is a simple three letter word: ASK! Ask, and continue to ask, no matter what anyone says—and no matter how often you hear "no."

Suppose They Say "No"

"No" only means "no." Nothing else should be attributed to it. Many people take "no" personally. They feel a personal rejection when another person says "no." Please, don't ascribe anything else to that little word. Everyone has a right to say "no." It is the other side of the "yes" coin. It has been said that the difference between good and bad salespeople is good ones don't take "no" personally (or seriously).

After hearing "no," they may ignore it and act as if the word was not said. Some people are devastated, and want to crawl into a corner and hide when they hear the word "no."

"No" is not an insult or defeat. It is another person exercising prerogatives. To some, "no" may feel like a slap in the face. If you feel this way, take a deep breath, count to three (or longer if necessary), and discuss the options and alternatives. You may want to bring in a mediator. Take a look at your options and move on.

Rejection Is the Worst

Rejection is the number one fear of human beings. We may have unfortunate habits from childhood that make us feel shame and humiliation. "No" is not a rejection unless we make it one. No one can reject us except ourselves. Unfortunately, most of us have been raised to believe "no" is one of the worst forms of rejection possible. We react in ways totally inappropriate to how we actually perceive ourselves to be.

If someone says they never want to see us again, this is not rejection. We can choose to perceive this, no matter what our feelings are toward that person, as one of the best favors they could do for us. Having this freedom is wonderful! We can now make room in our lives for those who truly see and appreciate us.

I am very much aware that I am a beautiful gem—one of a kind. I am also aware many people don't appreciate my kind of gem. I refuse to change myself to please other people. There are more than five billion people on this planet. When one of them says "goodbye," I may not like it, and may wish it were different. However, I realize there are four billion, nine hundred and ninety-nine million, nine hundred and ninety-nine thousand, nine hundred and ninety-nine others, some of whom would surely love and appreciate the many facets of my being.

How Not to Be A Dope

Loved and loving children are seldom victims of others' threatened rejections. Loving children and adults with high self-esteem seldom, if ever, respond to peer pressure. They know they are gems, and don't respond to threats or bullying of any kind.

A few years ago, one of our son's closest friends, Ray, was a heavy user of marijuana. His home life was in turmoil. He'd lived through a nasty divorce and inherited a rough, macho, dope-smoking stepfather who threatened physical violence and withdrawal of his love to control him.

Ray always had a joint, knew where to get one, and was almost totally "joint-oriented." He was more than delighted to share his stash with one and all. He often insisted his friends join him, even to the point of physical and emotional threats. In spite of this behavior, he was an incredibly delightful, sensitive young man. He attempted many times to force my sons to light up with him. He would offer in a friendly manner before resorting to force.

Helen and I had discussed every angle of every drug with all our children many times. They were given whatever information was available. Since drugs weren't a secret or "stolen pleasure" in our home, our children's curiosity about them didn't lead them to destruction.

Our son told Ray he didn't want any more dope. Ray launched an all-out attack. He used every trick in the book to persuade our son to change his mind.

Finally, our son sat Ray down, looked him square in the eyes, and said, "If our friendship, which I value very, very much, depends on my smoking pot, something I don't like or want to do, then I'm afraid I'll have to end our friendship. It's O.K. if you want to smoke, although I wish you wouldn't do it so heavily. It won't affect my love for you. But I am not going to smoke with you."

Ray was dumbfounded. No one had ever talked with him that way before. Their friendship flourished. Ray continued to smoke his beloved pot to excess. When his family moved out of town, Ray told our son he was, and would be, his best friend ever. He said he loved him very much. Unfortunately that kind of language is seldom spoken between teenage boys.

The above example demonstrates that *saying what we don't want is equally as important as asking for what we do* —and possibly more so at times. We love to say "yes" so we'll be thought of as "nice people." We loathe saying "no," for fear we won't. Often we fear people won't like us if we don't give them what they want. Remember, only a relationship based on honesty has any real power or potential. A relationship based on a lie is simply a lie.

To ask for what we want is honesty at its best. Not to ask is dishonest. It is a lie. To say "yes" when we don't want something or don't agree with something is also dishonest. However, we must be careful how we use this new power to say "no." We must answer our children's questions with pure honesty. Saying "no" to a child without good reasons instills fear and doubt in that child. Use "no" wisely and justly. Answers like "Just because I said so" are a copout.

If we are dishonest with our children, we teach them to lie, cheat, and be deceitful. When they lie we blame them—rather than acknowledge that we taught them how. If we don't want our children to lie, steal, or cheat, we must look to ourselves to see how much we've contributed to the unacceptable behavior. Friends, teachers, TV, movies, and everything else with which they come into contact influence our children's behavior. However, we are their prime instructors. They build the foundation for the rest of their lives on our examples and teachings. "Do as I say and not as I do" doesn't work with our children—or anybody else.

I beseech all parents to continually encourage your children to strive for honesty. Although we cannot force them to tell the truth, the choice is available. Light the path of honesty with your own bright examples. Every ray of light is needed, for the path is surrounded by darkness. In that darkness lurk the forces of the past, waiting to destroy personal potency and self-esteem.

14

Failure to Communicate

As a specialist in watching people communicate, I have noticed that most people talk *to* (and often *down to*) others instead of talking *with* them. It's as if others are too dumb or dull to really understand what we are saying. In transactional analysis, this is called a "Parent to Child" transaction. The "Stan Dale Law of Human Transactions" states: *"Every Parent to Child transaction will eventually elicit a Child to Parent negative feedback.* It may take decades, but eventually the Child will 'get back at' the offending Parent."

Humans relate to each other through communication. We do it in a variety of ways. The most common are verbalization (talk) and body language. Communicating is the way we make ourselves known to others by expressing what we want and what we need. When we relate to others, we connect our thoughts and ourselves to others. Sometimes we establish a truly intimate bridge, so our truer, "deeper" meanings (ones that may be obscured even from ourselves) are amplified and spotlighted.

Unfortunately parents and children seldom communicate and relate. Intimate communication is rare between any two people. Frightened and insecure, we don't want others to know the real us for fear they will reject us. Yet we long to be known on some levels. And because we are afraid, we seldom truly open up and make ourselves vulnerable. We keep ourselves trapped in inner conflict.

We seldom establish meaningful relationships with our children. Instead of being based on meaningful open communication, they are almost always superficial, order-giving/command-receiving relationships. Without realizing it, parents and teachers almost invariably talk down to children. We are like traffic cops to our children. We tell them when and where to go, how fast, and what the penalties are for breaking the parental laws.

Meanwhile we cry out to those we love to be more loving and more intimate. *For real intimacy to happen, we need to look at the way we communicate ourselves to others.* Do we really say what we feel? Are we clear in our communication, or do we obscure and confuse? Do we complicate, rather than simplify? Do we know when we are not heard or understood? If the answer to any or all of those questions is affirmative, perhaps it's time to reexamine our communication.

Communication and relationship are not taught in school. Yet children communicate and relate daily from the moment they wake up until they fall asleep. We grownups do the same. Where did we learn how? In our backward society, we teach things in reverse order of importance. Instead of teaching communication skills, we teach the "three R's." We do not prepare our children to communicate and relate to others. We do our best to learn by modeling what we see and hear others doing. They too learn by modeling others who in turn were taught no communication skills. We fumble our way through life, doing the best we know how. Each generation passes on its communication sickness to the next.

Let's break this life-damaging chain. If we began today to teach communication skills, I'm sure most parent-child problems, and other frustrations we experience, would begin to dissolve. The lack of cohesion in many families is really a function of a failure to communicate. It is time to establish a *meaningful* relationship with those we love. Communication is the key.

The Path to Potency

An important lesson to learn is: *to become more intimate is to become more vulnerable.* The paradox is **there is no way to be potent without being vulnerable, and there is no way to be vulnerable without being potent.** Think about this for a while. This took me many years to discover. In reading a book, the tendency is to rush through a sentence like that in a flash. Lay the book down, digest the information and return to reading. I contend that by digesting this one sentence you will find the source of a happy, fulfilled life.

We look everywhere but within ourselves. We try everything but the right thing to make us feel happier and more alive. We believe if we take the right pill, do the right thing, read the right books, or whatever, we will be happy and fulfilled.

Instead, we need do nothing, simply open the gate, unlock the locks, and let go. We must open our mouths to nourish ourselves. We must open our hearts to receive love. Until we are ready to open up and let go, we cannot create loving intimacy heart to heart. We are too busy protecting ourselves from all of those imagined and perceived fears.

Be vulnerable. What do we have to lose? Why do we keep a fort around our heart? What are we afraid of, especially when it comes to our own children? Our own flesh and blood. . . .

You Can't Be Too Open

Many parents worry that if they are too open, children will take advantage of them. Most young women feel the same way about men. As long as we are afraid someone will take advantage of us, there is little possibility of truly open, loving relationships. As long as we remain awake, and our minds have not been drugged, it is very difficult for us to be taken advantage of without our cooperation.

I assure you, if you talk with your children with understanding and love in your heart, you will never have to fear them taking advantage of you. When men go into battle, tyrannical officers are sometimes shot in the back. These are heartless commanders who talked down to their men and made them feel less than human. When leaders don't order their men to do anything they wouldn't do, and always talk to their men as if they are trusted, and treat them as intelligent human beings, they never need fear for their own safety or loss of authority. Men who follow good leaders will walk through fire and back for them.

At home, work, school, or play respect cannot be demanded. It must be earned and learned. It does not come automatically. When respect is given, it is almost always returned with fantastic dividends. The parent who demands respect from children is usually the first one to be "shot down" when a battle rages. The retaliation administered by the child may take many subtle forms, and take many years before coming to fruition. *I guarantee you, it will come.*

Open up your heart as widely as possible. Become as vulnerable as possible. Be as intimate with your children, lovers, and all others—just as you dream they might be with you. By doing so, you make it possible for them to open up to you. You create the possibility of a truly loving relationship. One of the best ways for this to happen is through open and honest communication.

Here are some communication guidelines to assist you:

1. *LISTEN!* Quiet your own self-talk and pay attention to what's being communicated.
2. *ASK!* Ask all of your questions. Be sincere. Be certain you totally understand what was said.
3. Don't make assumptions or take anything for granted. Communication is a two-way street. If there are more than two parties, a mediator may be required.
4. Be sure you understand the meaning behind the words. It takes time for even the best communicators to understand the intended meanings of the words every time.
5. Be sure to pause before you respond. Many a disaster has occurred because of one hastily spoken word.
6. Use "I" messages. Own your own thoughts and feelings. Don't ascribe them to another person. (I feel, I think, I want, etc.) Many people think by using "you" messages they won't appear self-centered. (For example, "You make me angry" instead of "I make myself angry.") In essence,

they don't want to take personal responsibility.

7. Clarify. Do not leave a communication dangling. Be sure both parties fully understand each other. Do not assume this to be so. It is better to be redundant than to be misunderstood.

8. Write down or record the communication. If it's important enough, and the situation lends itself, write down at least the important points to avoid confusion and distortion over time.

9. Avoid sermons or lectures, especially to children. Boring sermons and lectures alienate your listeners.

10. Don't presume to know it all or to be infallible. Everyone makes mistakes. No one is always right. There is your truth, your child's truth, and the whole truth, which is usually larger than either individual truth.

11. Own your own opinions. Know that your opinions are just fantasies, a creation of your mind and its particular programming.

12. Remember, *all communication is nothing more than making sure the other person or people get your message.* It is you showing them the pictures from inside your mind, without distortion. If the picture is fuzzy, don't expect to be understood. Clear up the picture!

All languages are almost totally devoid of the words adequate to describe our feelings and thoughts. Sometimes our thoughts are not clear or distinct—even to us. Attempting to communicate is like an artist attempting to find the right shade of color to convey the appropriate texture or tone. Despite many mixes or blends, the end result may still be off a tad. However, if the artist and the speaker persevere, they can at least come very close.

Like the tireless artist, the active parent attempts to find the best words to make the picture clear for both the parent and the child. After all, if you have difficulty expressing yourself clearly at your age, what do you expect from a child?

Everyone wants to be heard. Despite the difficulty in expressing ourselves, we want to be understood. Possibly the reason we communicate so poorly is that speech is our most recently acquired trait. Our fore-bears probably used basic hand signals and grunts. Relative to the total span of evolution, we have only recently emerged from the cave.

As a professional communicator, I am painfully aware of how difficult it is for people to speak in public. More than once, my college speech class students have fainted, collapsed, become weak in the knees or sick to their stomachs when required to deliver a talk or a speech. The assignment was simple, and usually about something familiar to them. For most it turned out to be pure torture. Only after much nurturing, support, and patience, were these students able to get up and talk to others.

The same cure worked for students who stammered and stuttered. These speech aberrations are not natural human conditions. They are direct products of fear and anxiety. The initial "glitch" took place as the child was attempting to be heard. Eventually it became a full-blown habit. After just one semester of *knowing* it was possible to eliminate stammering and stuttering, many students either abandoned or modified their speech patterns.

When it comes to childrearing, we are all amateurs, even the so-called "experts." We are all feeling our way. As far as I can see, there are no Einsteins of child rearing on the horizon. After many centuries of erecting "towers of babble," we have inherited many confusing and outdated injunctions and imperatives. We feel pulled, pushed, ripped, and torn apart about what should and shouldn't be done. I implore us not to give up, throw our hands up in disgust, and return to the old ways because it's easy. It may be easy and it may also be trouble. Change takes commitment, for old neuronal pathways run as deep as the Grand Canyon.

On occasion it may be advisable to take a break, even a vacation away from the children. When you come back refreshed and centered, you can throw yourself into active parenting with a new commitment and fervor.

Remember it is O.K. to make mistakes. Don't punish yourself or your children if you do. Once a mistake is realized, don't hesitate to communicate your intent to change your behavior. It is never too late.

Even a small amount of quality time relating and communicating can pay off tenfold. Return to your commitment to be an active parent. Then you and your children will have a firm platform upon which to stand. You need not sink into the quicksands of misunderstanding: fear, confusion, and anxiety. Always remember to communicate your truth!

15

Sex, Nudity, and Dating

In our sex-crazy culture, one of the most difficult things to talk or write about with intelligence and openness is sex. In spite of technological advances, our attitudes toward sex have been confused and obscured, not really changing very much for over five thousand years.

Americans in particular continue to be naive and ignorant about sex. Where are we supposed to learn? Surely not in school. Sex education courses? Most of them are farces, if not downright dangerous, injurious, and counterproductive. Where, then? Unfortunately, not in the home. Too few parents have the knowledge, and many are afraid to talk to their children about this still "taboo" subject.

Sex + Lies = Disaster

As a sexologist for half my life, I find it increasingly more difficult, as time goes by, to hear the same horror stories over and over again with only minor variations. I've heard from thousands of people about how *their lives have been virtually ruined by the lack of, or downright poor, sex education.* The horrors range from poor self-esteem, wrecked homes and marriages, disease, unwanted pregnancies, and botched abortions to rape, suicide, and murder. We as a society refuse to grow up and deal with sex honestly and openly. The lies we have unknowingly perpetuated over the centuries are coming back to haunt us.

As radical as it may sound, if we can begin to tell the truth, we can halt the spread in this country of virtually all sexually transmitted diseases (STDs), including AIDS. First, we must pull our heads out of the sand and look the truth square in the face. We need an all-out media blitz, including television, radio, newspapers, and magazines. We would need to gear up the public health forces and have them establish mobile units in the field, as they do with bloodmobiles and T.B. testers. In addition, we need school-wide programs with knowledgeable sexologists speaking to children of all ages. We need an all-out frontal attack on the ignorance and fear that perpetuate the diseases. At the same time, we can most likely do away with millions of unwanted and dangerous teenage pregnancies that threaten the lives, the quality of life, and the well-being of our young people.

However, the forces of ignorance and fear are unforgiving. In their campaign, *existing* human lives are unimportant. These forces are willing to let millions fall victim to punitive actions. Out of ignorance and fear, we tell our children (and others), don't fool around with sex outside of marriage. When illness or pregnancy occurs, out of ignorance and fear we say they should suffer the consequences—even if this means destroying their lives and the lives of others. This is an antihuman, unforgiving, and punitive ideology. Unfortunately, it pervades the very fiber and fabric of this country.

We treat sex like it is something dirty. We use the words "sex" and "violence" together as if they were interchangeable. Public educators are loath to teach sex education courses because of potential parental and church condemnation. If they dare broach the subject at all, it is usually treated as biology or slid into a home economics course.

Our mass media, with very few exceptions, exploits sex and uses it to titillate, excite, and ridicule. Movies with pure gut-wrenching violence are rated "PG" or "PG-13" (parental guidance); with nudity, "R" (restricted); and with explicit sex, "NC-17" formerly "X" (no one under 18 admitted). In effect, they say violence, no matter how explicit and gruesome, is acceptable to be seen by those under 18; sex, no matter how beautiful and tender, is not okay.

Then Sex Is Okay?

Can someone please tell me why the very function that brought all of us to life on this planet is treated with such panic, hysteria, fear, and loathing? Why is sex in such disfavor? Why is it hidden from the young, and treated by grown, mature people as something mysterious, vile, dirty, something to cause fear and shame? Many years of research have yet to yield definitive answers.

One of the most logical answers is the biblical injunction to have sex only for procreation. Why did the writers of the Bible state it that way? What was the foundation for this injunction? A notable interpretation (and there are many interpretations of everything in the Bible) is the ancients feared the human race would be destroyed if "man wasted his seed." This is called the "Sin of Onan," one of the worst possible sins.

They had no microscopes back then, and were not aware that men have no *seeds*. Men have sperm. Up to half a billion of them are released in a healthy young man's single ejaculation. There is enough sperm in every ten ejaculations to repopulate the planet. This was unknown in biblical times. People probably feared the human race would literally and figuratively "go down the tubes." They may have reasoned that, if man had seeds, the supply might be limited. And once they were all used, then what?

They did know about masturbation, nocturnal emissions, and also almost zero fertility during the menses. So, fearing the end of the human race, they said, "Thou shalt not!" They didn't know how to say, "Look guys, procreate, have a couple of babies first to make sure the human race survives, then have sex for recreation." Such knowledge was unavailable and therefore unspoken. All they knew was, "Thou shalt not, under the threat of severe retribution." (A sense of humor appears to be lacking in this way of thinking.)

We are the victims of over five thousand years of "thou shalt nots." Even on this overpopulated planet, we are still controlled by the imperative, "Go ye forth and multiply." When there was only a handful of people on the planet, this may have been practical. Now, we are over five billion who are depleting our environmental future.

Teach It Right or Else

One of the worst crimes is the perpetuation of ignorance and fear. These twin grim-reapers of humanity must be exposed. It is time to strip away their hooded cloaks and scythes with the spotlight of truth.

We must begin to teach our children freely. We need to be aware every moment that everything we do and don't do, say and don't say, is recorded by our children's brains. Although children may not totally understand what is recorded in those microscopic memory banks, it nevertheless controls their thoughts and behaviors for the rest of their lives.

Many people make a claim for sex education in the home. They say they don't want outsiders teaching their kids. The primary school for sex education is, indeed, the home. Everything experienced there is education. Most of the teaching is nonverbal, so we are constantly telling them about sex, marriage, family, sensuality, and more. Messages are transmitted through touch or lack of touch, a kiss or no kiss, and how, where, and when we do or don't express ourselves to each other. For example when Mommy and Daddy go into the bedroom and close the door, that simple act (and what is said or not said) teaches volumes about sex. Children learn their attitudes from how we think about and handle the subject of sex.

Do we openly tell our children we are going into the bedroom to have sex, or do we disguise the truth? It is very important to be honest with our children about what is going on behind that door. Otherwise, it can be blown way out of proportion by their fertile young minds. We must explain sex to them, let them know what the sounds are about, if there are any. All this information helps them develop a healthy understanding about sex. We can gently tell our children what sex feels like, honestly and objectively. The way we relate our feelings and experiences of sex lays the foundation for our children's own sex lives. If we convey a horror story, our children's sex lives may also be horrific.

If and when your children ask to watch you have sex, good luck. Many a so-called liberated person has collapsed like so much jelly with that request. How you handle it, and what you say and do, tells your children much more about sex than anything you could plan to communicate. If you feel comfortable about sex, then the answer is natural and unforced. If you don't, your fears may be imprinted on their brains for all time.

If you are embarrassed to talk about sex, you might wish to do a little self-questioning. Where does your embarrassment originate? Do you act that way about anything else? If so, why? How did you receive a sex education?

I caution you not to feel compelled to do anything you are unprepared to handle. Many people, in attempting to be progressive and sexually open, take on more than they can handle and may even cause damage. *Allow no one to force you to take actions against your better judgment.* If you feel uncomfortable about anything, let your children know. Be totally honest. It will help them tremendously.

A good alternative to having children watch is to rent some motion pictures on the subject.* You might also locate a sexologist in your area so you, your family, club, school, etc., can be introduced to a sex-positive, intelligent educational program. This is an excellent way to give other parents the opportunity of forming a support group so you can all resource each other. This is an ideal way to teach your children at home.

In addition children learn about sex by the way we treat the members of each gender. We talk differently to boys and girls. We respond to them differently in many subliminal ways. Each gender is treated more or less gentle, more or less sexy and come-on-ish, etc. Do we say girls are pretty, soft, and sweet, while tossing the boys around? Do we dress and make-up little girls,

---

* The Multi-Media Resource Center, 1523 Franklin Street, San Francisco, CA 94109, (415) 928-1133, has an excellent selection of films, books, slides, and other teaching aids. They can also refer you to sexologists in your area.

while letting the boys "be boys"? *This, too, is sex education!*

Please Speak English

What if from the very beginning, children could hear the truth about their bodies and the way they function. Suppose we use the correct words for their body parts, at the same time that they are learning to say Mommy and Daddy. Nothing about the human body is weird or dirty. The words and names we use to describe it and its functions must be stated as openly, and as matter of factly, as we would say anything else. Why do we reduce ourselves to baby talk like "doo doo," "pee pee," "ca ca," "wee wee," etc.

It is important to talk about the genitals and their potential for good and bad feelings without distorting either. Genitals are not dirty. References to sex as dirty can inhibit our children's growth. We must talk openly and fully, to boys and girls alike, about menstruation, wet dreams, and all of the phenomena that accompany physical maturation.

Children have the right to know the pleasures their genitals can provide them, for free, for the rest of their lives. When they begin to explore their genitals (and most start long before they can understand words), let them do so. After all, what are they doing wrong? The same applies to playing doctor or nurse. Let them experiment, explore, and discover their bodies. It is normal and healthy. Besides being fun, they learn far more than they ever get from textbooks. This will not turn them into sex maniacs or rapists. Experimentation is totally natural. Depriving them of these opportunities does more damage than anything they learn from each other. They are simply being good scientists.

Long before your children go on their first date, tell them about contraception and the responsibilities of each one involved. Contraception is the responsibility of both parties, not just the female. Both must be equally prepared. There is no 100 percent sure method. There are too many chances for pregnancy. Even with contraception, all probabilities and possibilities must be considered.

Abortion is an inappropriate and expensive form of birth control. Planned Parenthood is a good resource for information on contraception. On the outside chance that conception does take place, all contingency plans should be in place ahead of time. If pregnancy does occur, it is important to be calm and clear headed. Young people must be given all the input, information, and support possible. At the same time, we must recognize the ultimate decisions are theirs.

Being Responsible

In addition to contraception, speak with your children about responsible sex. AIDS (acquired immune deficiency syndrome) and other STDs (sexually transmitted diseases) are very real threats. Children must be made fully aware of the risks they are taking. Fortunately, with awareness and proper precautions, it is possible to minimize the risk. Many high schools have effective AIDS education programs. Often, however, young people (and adults as well) have an "it can't happen to me" attitude. Unfortunately, the AIDS virus is not so selective. It can happen to anyone who does not practice responsible sex.

While I do not intend to make light of STDs, I want to defuse some of the craziness surrounding them. The common cold is the best-known STD around. I'm sure few of us would advocate no contact with kissing and touching other human beings in order to avoid getting colds. Yet most people, including the medical profession, are a bit irrational about STDs. STDs are no different from any other disease. They do, however, receive considerable negative press.

Why do we treat STDs differently from others? Is it because they are contracted during an act of intimacy? With the exception of AIDS, they are nowhere near as dangerous as many other diseases. AIDS and herpes are the only STDs that don't have a cure.

We continue to decry the scourge of venereal disease as vile and sleazy. Our attitude toward these diseases helps to perpetuate them. As I said earlier, if we can eliminate ignorance and fear, we can do away with almost all STDs (including AIDS). First, we must learn not to punish and exact revenge upon those we love for engaging in sexual activity.

It is time we neutralize sex words. Our children need to know that through ignorance, people use sex words as curses and put-downs. Children must learn not to imitate them and perpetuate this ignorance. Sex words are harsh-sounding only because of the anti-sexual attitudes of our ancestors. They need to learn that *the sex act or anything that is connected with it is not to be made fun of or demeaned.* All the negative connotations attached to sex erode our children's self-confidence. Factual, straightforward words and attitudes nurture and support them.

When talking about sex and relationships, it is important to discuss the difference between infatuation, turn-on, and love. Many people, especially young people, think infatuation and sexual turn-on, because they are so "juicy," mean love. Our children need to know that infatuation and turn-on are nature's way of releasing the juices to prepare the body for sex. Even though the feelings can be overwhelming at times, it is not necessary to act on those feelings with another person. Although they may hear bells, the bells may not be of the wedding variety.

Children should be taught it is perfectly O.K. to have sex with themselves, if they feel it is appropriate. Self-pleasuring teaches them about their sexual responses. They learn to better understand their preferences, and can better tell them to partners in the future.

Today there is a lot of peer pressure to have sex with others at early ages (even in elementary school). Because it's the popular thing to do, children must learn to make appropriate choices for themselves. Only they know when it's time for them. Children need to be able to communicate their needs and wants without giving way to pressures of their peers.

Sex Does Not Equal Love

It is important to convey the differences between sex and love. The two do not always go together. Even though everything is best done with love, including washing the toilet bowl and the dishes, there are times when it's O.K. to have sex for sex's sake. Love does not always have to be present. Although we euphemistically translate "making love" as the sex act, love may or may not be involved.

Finally, be sure your children understand that many people seek love through sex. Although this may be one route love travels, sex does not necessarily produce love, nor vice versa. As a matter of fact, sexual activity is often *an avoidance of love and intimacy.*

Unfortunately, many people have difficulty with these unhealthy attitudes and feelings toward love and intimacy because of their ignorance and how they learned (or rather, did not learn) about sex.

Sex is as natural as eating, sleeping, and breathing. To treat it as alien is to invite disaster. Of the nearly 30,000 people who have participated in my sex workshops over the past 20-plus years, the vast majority had previously endured awful suffering because of a limited and warped sex education or lack of any sex education at all. What needless misery, horror, and expense so many have suffered because of ignorance perpetuated from the past.

No matter what your background and sexual history, you can learn to talk openly with your children. Let them know about your past and your experiences, and how it was for *you.* Tell them each person may feel entirely different, even in an almost identical situation. If you have had pains and problems, let them know. Don't hide or sugarcoat anything. Let them know about your wide variety of experiences. Call upon friends and other family members to add their own. The more the young people know, the more awareness they have. And the more awareness, the better their chances for a secure and happy life in all domains, including sex.

Admit when you don't know the answer to a question, and set out together to find the answer. Let the youngsters teach you. Their experiences are unique. Give them the opportunity and satisfaction of teaching their elders. It strengthens the bond and intimacy between you.

Unfortunately, it is imperative that your children be aware that different people respond and react differently to the topic of sex. They must know it's sad that society sometimes punishes honesty, especially where sex is concerned. Let your children know that what you say or do in your family may be considered evil, sinful, and dirty by the less informed. Children who learn to understand and respect other people's way of thinking avoid much difficulty.

Nudity

I highly encourage nudity, in and out of the home, for many reasons. The most important reason is that it is honest. *Nudity promotes honesty.* In spite of all the outdated religious and Freudian beliefs to the contrary, nudity is natural and healthy. It does not promote Oedipus complexes, or any other sexual desires. The contrary is closer to the truth. Nudity practiced in the home becomes natural. Children really relate to nudity. That's how they entered this world.

In our family, total nudity has been practiced almost from the very beginning. Along with my four sons, the other nudists we know are some of the healthiest, most humane people we have met. One of my daughters grew up in the South with her religious mother. She came to visit one summer and joined us at a nudist camp. She had never been nude in front of others before. After about an hour, she said she had never felt so at ease and comfortable with her body, clothed or unclothed. She said she loved the way the men and boys looked in her eyes when they talked, rather than being riveted to her breasts and acting like sex-starved madmen. She is a beautiful woman, inside and out. Unfortunately, she is continually harassed about her body. To her surprise after a full day of romping like a wood nymph in close contact with many men, not one acted as she would have expected. Respect for the human body can be the norm, not the exception.

Have you ever been nude in front of other people? Would you like to try it? Great! A perfect place to visit is a nudist club or retreat. If you have children, make it a family outing. Create a fun day to be like all of the other creatures on the planet: nude. Isn't it odd that we are the only living creatures that abhor our natural state? We have to wear clothing to cover our naturalness? *To me, an unnatural sex act is having to dress to go swimming.* Now *that's* perverse!

If you want to experience honesty in the form of nudity, ask yourself a few questions: Why does being nude make you feel uncomfortable? What, if anything, do you want to do about it? What is wrong with nudity? What do you have to hide? What are you afraid someone will see? Why is a piece of cloth more virtuous than that astounding work of art, the human body?

How exciting the body is, no matter how it looks. No two bodies are alike. Like snowflakes, each is distinctly different. Do you feel that you are too fat, too skinny, too big, too tall, or your stretch marks are ugly? You have been thoroughly brainwashed. Human bodies in all of their sizes, shapes, and configurations are the way they're meant to be. They are simply human bodies.

One reason there is so much sexual dissatisfaction is that most younger people think bodies should resemble *Playboy, Penthouse,* or *Playgirl* centerfolds. They seldom if ever have an an opportunity to look at *real* bodies. When they do look, they are often disappointed because in growing up they didn't see *real* naked bodies with all of their so-called inherent differences. Centerfolds have been air brushed to take out the blemishes, the realities of the human body.

Your children must make their own choice around nudity. It is important not to force them. Older children have learned society's rules and regulations, and sometimes even two or three-year-olds are reluctant to go nude. When clothing is the norm, they adapt. All the craziness about sex and nudity disappear when children are taught from birth that nudity is natural. In learning to speak, little children rapidly learn what they hear. They can learn with incredible speed whatever languages are part of their everyday environment. Learning becomes more difficult as they get older if they must first unlearn old ideas and behaviors. This applies to everything children experience and learn, even ignorance and fear.

It is wise to be cautious when introducing nudity to children past the age of three or four. Their basic habits and socialization have been pretty well established. First, talk about what you intend to do, then demonstrate your sincerity and comfort with the subject. Ask them how they might feel if they could walk around the house for a while without clothes. Ask if they would mind if you do the same thing. If they have objections, talk about them. Let them suggest possible options and alternatives. Ask if they want to discuss the idea with other people or read about it. There are many good books available for children that deal with sex and nudity.

If they still prefer to wear clothes, and have you wear yours, fine. That is their right. However, you have rights, too. You may choose to establish a set time each day to be nude. Let them know that time.

If they prefer not to be around at that time, you can assist them in finding another place to be. Of course, tell them why you want to be nude, and answer all of their questions. It is important for everyone to be comfortable and to have all needs met and honored.

Force in any form will only alienate your children. If they don't want to do a certain thing or go some place you think they should, please remember the question "Do I want to be treated that way?"

Dating

When it comes to dating, there is no such thing as "the right age." Only parents who are uptight and untrusting are concerned about their children dating too young. Dating is nothing more than two or more people getting together. Leave the who, when, how, etc., entirely to those involved.

If no "big deal" is made of dating, it is a perfectly natural event. Avoid the hoopla and trauma some people experience when it comes time for their children to date. If parents were more natural in their attitudes about dating, the craziness we experience around the so-called "dating game" would disappear.

When adults attempt to date, they often have traumatic, nerve-shattering experiences. Much unhappiness and fear could be alleviated if they had only been allowed to be natural in their younger years. We fear our children will have sex and imagine all sorts of horrible things happening. We don't trust our children and treat them like criminals in the making. We force them into secrecy and teach them to lie, cheat, and steal. For some children, this is a matter of survival with their unskillful, warped parents. If they don't take

131

the initiative, no matter the consequences, they never get anything they want. This does not mean I condone any of these actions. I am simply reporting the reasons.

Many parents act as if they are the F.B.I. and children foreign agents: sneaky, underhanded, and waiting to destroy the family. *Parents who don't trust their children really don't trust themselves.* They impose their own not O.K. feelings on their children. Then they wonder why their children act the way they do.

Children, like adults, respond poorly to all sorts of embarrassing questions. Trust them, even if it is difficult. Ask them if they need any support, or information from you, and then give them the freedom to learn and grow. If you feel nervous and upset, tell them why. Let them know how it is for you. Take caution not to lay your heavy trip on your children's heads.

Arbitrary and unilateral curfew laws are confining and ineffectual. Discuss what your children feel is an appropriate time for them to return home. Ask them to call if they feel they need more time. Let them know the call is not designed to pry into their affairs, or due to a lack of trust. Tell them you appreciate being included in any change of plans so you can adjust your life accordingly. If they don't call, even after this agreement, please don't lose your cool, get angry, and punish them. Ask them what happened, without taking the role of F.B.I. agent. Accept their answer. It is amazing how many legitimate things can happen. Like yourself, they too can forget. After all, when you were out under the stars, did you think of Mother and Father and a telephone? I hope not.

Take your negative fantasies in hand and turn them into positive ones. They are simply *your* fears, *your* negative fantasies, and *your* training. Remember, you have taught your children well. Give them an opportunity to show they have learned. Learn to relax and trust.

Naturosexuality

Before closing this chapter, a word to parents who fear that their children might be bisexual or homosexual. All sex is natural as long as it is consensual. Almost all other forms of life on this planet engage in same-sex activity. I have coined a word that I hope eventually will be accepted by the masses: *"naturosexuality," naturally sexual. We are all naturosexual.* Because we express only one facet of our sexuality, that does not make that one right. It is simply the generally accepted societal way. Who set that norm?

If your children enjoy same-sex activity, please don't try to change them or make them wrong. This is their natural sexual preference. As long as our children love and enjoy themselves, why are we so concerned? If you fear that God will punish them, because the Bible says it is a sin, then please leave it up to God. You are not God's surrogate. You are neither judge nor executioner. Your job, as a loving parent, is to simply love your child: unquestioningly and unconditionally. You may have your opinions and your preferences. But to tell your children you hate them for their choice is to demean the beauty of the universe, and of love.

Except for procreation, what is all the craziness surrounding our sexual choices about? Why is it considered sick to enjoy homosexual love? Granted, it is not the norm, but why hate people who love? Hatred abounds through much of our society. If people are suspected of being homosexual, it is often considered sufficient grounds for every inhumane act from firing them from a job to extreme physical violence against their person. All across the country "macho" men torment those they suspect of being gay—at times, to the point of death. What gross injustice do we humans bring on one another?!!

Many homosexuals also enjoy heterosexual experiences, and many become parents. Sex roles and stereotypes are learned from the very beginning, and some factors may be inborn. We have little scientific proof either way. Little children have no preference as to whether someone of the same sex or the opposite sex is loving them. They merely enjoy feeling loved. Why make them suffer when they are grown if they choose not to conform?

I implore you, simply love your children, no matter what their sexual preference. Let them know you are always willing to learn. Tell them nothing they choose to do will alienate you and cause you to take your love away.

Remember, our society has a monumental history of sexual repression, oppression, and ignorance to overcome. You will need all the help and support you can get.

16

Creating Family

Allies make marvelous partners. This is true whether we are talking about countries, friends, children, or the next-door neighbor. In our society of nuclear families, allies have become difficult to find and maintain. We have become isolated units—islands in a sea of people—with few, if any, safe harbors. Most of us have moved many miles from the family and friends of our youth. We find ourselves alone and lonely. Many times we are afraid to venture forth to establish a bridge with the next little island. We fear the bridge will collapse, or the natives will be hostile. We have become prisoners of our own islands.

The gross alienation in this country began with the industrial revolution, when people left their farms or homelands to venture forth to the cities to work in the new factories. What appeared to be the promise of new wealth and fortune turned out, for most people, to be an empty hope. The wife became the slave of the home and the husband the slave of the factory. When (and if) they had time to be with each other, they were usually tired and bleary-eyed. Many became little more than stranger/zombies simply living with each other as battling roommates. Whenever there was time available for a little intimacy, entertainment, or diversion, they were either too alienated or too pooped. As a result they turned further inward, and became more isolated. They were hardened strangers to each other. All they accomplished, by and large, was to get further in debt, more angry, and more dissatisfied. Their possessions took precedence over their relationships. They found it harder to relate to one another. Increasing divorce left single parents who came to rely on their children for emotional support. Increasingly, children became a substitute for the missing spouse.

The extended families of the past provided a base of support and nurturing. Now virtually nonexistent, in many ways they resembled collectives and communes, in that the members provided each other with mutual support. However, extended families had their dark side. Some were little more than mini-dictatorships, headed by tyrannical despots who issued commands and made demands with little regard for the individuals concerned. In spite of this, there was a feeling of community—of belonging. This sense of family is often missing in today's isolated nuclear families.

Because children fill the void left by the collapse of the extended unit, they are sometimes expected to limit their associations. Parents may be suspicious of them and their friends. We may limit the amount of time they spend with "strangers." We teach our children to have their needs met within the confines of the family. Unfortunately, stranger/zombies with no zest for life are poor resources for bright, inquisitive, restless, playful children.

Grandparents, those veritable fountains of everything good from the past (from home-baked pies to Grandpa's homespun stories), enrich the lives of our children. However, in many cases opportunities to visit are limited. The same is true of aunts, uncles, and cousins, all of whom have much to add to the patchwork-crazy-quilt fabric of life. They are often virtual strangers whose visits are squeezed into a hectic pace of life.

Do We Really Want to Be Nuked?

The nuclear family is a poor substitute for what we humans desperately desire—a full-blown family tree and a magnificent, goody-laden Christmas tree. We want a family tree to shelter us from the storms of life. We do not want our families to be a prison. We want our families to be a place we are perfectly free to leave, without fear or guilt, whenever the need or desire arises.

Helen, our sons, and I have discovered that we can have the benefits of the extended family of the past—without the brambles and burrs that sometimes accompany these relationships. We have found ways to make this balance available in the here and now. It is there for the asking.

Together we have established an "intentional non-oppressive family" that, at last count, numbered about 200 people. They are the supportive, nurturing, loving, intelligent, like-minded people who have transcended the invisible barrier of just being friends and acquaintances. These are people who exhibit pure heart-to-heart love, concern, and intimacy for each other, and for us. They have become closer to us than most members of our biological family. These are people who know and accept us, and the rest of our family, with unconditional love. There isn't a thing they wouldn't do for us, or we for them. We need never fear that one of them would "stab us in the back" or do anything negative or counterproductive to our welfare.

The culling process of finding family members has been going on now for over ten years. We are totally satisfied that we are a family, not just unrelated friends. Think of everything positive that means family to you. That is what these people are to us. I trust them with everything I have, including my life and the welfare and well-being of my children. Some of them have been, and still are, surrogate parents to our children.

Children with access to the minds and thoughts (as well as the stroking) of only one set of parents have a very limited space in which to grow. They are denied the possibility of a richly lush Garden of Eden. *How arrogant we parents are to believe we are the only ones qualified to raise our children.* Each person is a huge reservoir of experiences, thoughts, information, and physical contact that enrich the lives of our children— and all with whom they come in contact.

We never have to worry about dictators, tyrants, or rip-off artists in this family. We continually come together to reinforce our love and our belief in each other. Like family, none of us stands on ceremony with another. We accept each other unconditionally, just the way we are. That doesn't mean we don't dislike some of the things each of us may do or say, but that never diminishes the love we feel for each other.

Periodically we have family meetings at which we share what we like and dislike about ourselves and each other. This exercise in total honesty serves to further strengthen the bonds that unite us. Sometimes at these sessions (which may last an entire weekend) each person has an opportunity to face each of the other members of the family. Each of us can share anything he or she has to say without any reply or interruption, or any fear of rebuke, alienation, rejection, judgment, or abandonment. This gives each of us the opportunity to share what doesn't work for us in our relationships with other members of the family, and to take responsibility for doing something about it. Each comment is stated with nurturing love and concern, never wielded like a bat or sword.

By the time this process is through, there is never a lack of things to talk about. Our parties and fun times are never phony or filled with trite, trivial conversation. At some meetings we get together to update who and what we are and what we believe and think. Ours is a conscious, intentional family, not a random collection of individuals who happen to be connected by blood. We are together because of a shared base of beliefs. And because our beliefs change as we change and grow, it is important that we keep each other up-to-date.

Democracy Begins in the Family

No one in our family is the leader, and each person has the opportunity to become facilitator of our meetings, or to take the floor as often as is wanted or necessary. It amazes me how family members take responsibility for their needs, wants, and desires, and for solving the problems that may enter their lives. We do not take advantage of each other or the group, except in the positive sense of that phrase.

No matter how small or large your family, the above may serve as a model of what is available to you and those you love. It is extremely easy to form an extended family. List your friends and acquaintances, and compile a list of those with whom you'd like to be more intimate. Then broach the question of extended family status with them. It may astound you how receptive many of them will be, especially when they realize that the benefits are infinite, and the love abounding.

It is also possible to start this kind of family by putting personal ads in your local newspaper, or a publication from your place of work, your church, or the clubs and organizations to which you belong. It is even possible to get on various radio and TV talk shows to advance the idea and ask for potential family members. The culling process can be one of the most exciting experiences of your life. And be sure to include the children. Remember, they are your family, too.

17

The Loving People

As stated earlier, this book is about love: pure, unadulterated, unconditional love. Yet, to talk about love in this manner, at this time in our cultural history, is akin to speaking a foreign language.

I am hooted and laughed at when I say, *"I absolutely love all human beings."* True, I may not always like their behavior. Nonetheless, *I love them*—the human being.

People differ in education, habits, finances, etc. But in the important things in life, we are alike. We all have a heart that beats, we have human feelings, and we are all trying to make our lives work using the skillful or unskillful programming we picked up over the years. We are all wounded children wanting to heal ourselves.

Whenever I meet a person, no matter how they look or what they do, I immediately see the baby and child they once were. They cannot hide. I know them for what they truly are: a perfect human being. I also recognize any behavior they act out is only one of two things: either an expression of love or a cry for love.

Unfortunately, it is a rare person who can truly love, purely, unabashedly, and unconditionally. I contend it is almost impossible to find more than a handful of humankind who haven't been so brainwashed and conditioned that they can love without letting anything get in the way, and without saying, "Yes, but. . . ."

I am asking for each human being to be willing to unconditionally love each and every other human being. It is not necessary to like what others do, yet we can love them: the child inside, the person crying out for love. I ask that we reevaluate our course. Where are we headed? Are we rushing headlong into disaster?

We are already too close to the precipice. Why? Because we are suspicious and distrustful of all of those "others" out there. We are suspicious and hateful of those who don't look, act, and sound like us. We are suspicious of those we have been taught to hate. And they are suspicious of us. As the Chinese proverb says, "If we keep on going in the direction we're headed, we'll get where we're going."

Hate may be too strong a word for some. Most people deny they hate anyone. I ask you to examine yourself. Are you open and loving to everyone? Are you truly open to those you claim to love? Are you really open and honest with your spouse, your lover, your children, your parents? Can you welcome a Russian, Chinese, or Vietnamese into your home and your arms? How do you treat a "spick," "wop," "greaser," "kike," "nigger," "honky," "slant," or "gook"? How about someone who is old or sick? Can you love a Catholic, Jew, Protestant, Hare-Krishna, or "Moonie"? Can you hug a retarded person or a homosexual?

I'm sure if you search hard and long enough, you can find at least one. It's that *one* that concerns me. One unloving thought is enough to thwart us from becoming truly loving people. When you cannot or will not love another person, what you are saying is that you cannot or will not love a part of yourself. You are as much a part of "other" people as they are a part of us. *What you hate in others is what you hate most in yourself.*

You realize, of course, no one is born hating themselves. This is a learned behavior. We must unlearn
what we've been taught. We must stop hating ourselves and others. We must stop acting as our own
worst enemies.

In this urban society, we have learned to distrust
others all the time. Many of us are prisoners in our
own homes. We are afraid to venture out and go
anywhere or meet anyone. The elderly are even more
frightened and victimized than most. They are easy
prey. Most stay home, glued to their television sets,
and go out only under duress.

We allow a handful of people to intimidate a whole
nation. We buy guns, burglar alarms, security systems,
and killer dogs at an alarming rate and cost. Many
people, if they go out at all, are armed with everything
from guns and knives to mace and tear gas. Gun sales
have skyrocketed. It's becoming the "Wild West" all
over again. We are walking arsenals. We become
more fearful and paranoid by the minute.

If someone approaches us on the street, we recoil
like a rattler ready to strike. Theaters and amusement
centers struggle to stay alive. This is due not only to
the economy, but also to fear. The majority of people
are content to stay home and watch their television
sets and play with their video games.

As a society, we are isolating ourselves, winding
inward like the mainspring of a watch. The spring is
so taut it soon may break.

The hectic pace is becoming more and more frantic.
People rush around, with little consideration as to what
all the rush is about. They have no idea where they
are going. The rush to accumulate things is more manic

than ever before. What are we grabbing? What has happened? Where are we headed?

There Is Only Now

I have never pretended to see the future. I am proud to consider myself a "here and now-ist." I live as fully as possible in the present, and extract every bit of juice out of my life today. I don't live in the past or the future, so I cannot say where we are headed. I seek a keen sense of history to gain a greater sense of balance. I believe there is no one alive who knows where we are headed, or what the future holds. We can only speculate and fantasize.

I find being in the now 99 percent of the time, allows me to remain totally potent. I can affect everything I encounter within reason, rather than be *at the effect of* my environment. I suggest this attitude can serve you equally well. Give up fantasies about the future and what might happen to you "if." Take control of your life now! *Take a risk! If you don't, you are already dead.*

Love, live, and enjoy life. Don't allow yourself to become a nonperson. Yes, you can be mugged, raped, or even killed. These are always possibilities and no one wants any of these negative things to happen. They are potential threats in our society. I'm sure there have been times during history when it was even worse. Today, through the miracle of modern technology, we know more about these injustices sooner. We quickly know when someone has shot a gun thousands of miles away. Because of television and satellite technology, we suffer a negative information overload. We are scared to death. "We are scared" is a negative fantasy.

"To death" means a cessation of life. We fantasize, and we cease living.

You can't reach out and love someone if you are locked in a closet or a silo. You have to get outside first. Other people need to know you are alive and willing to live before you die. You are emotionally dead unless you do.

The person who fears death dies a million times. The person who makes peace with death dies but once. As is always the case, the choice is up to you. Do you sit in your warm, safe prison and die, or do you venture out and dive into life? Do you live and squeeze every last drop out of this precious life, or are you content to let it slip away?

If you choose to live (and I sincerely hope this is your choice), live fully and openly. Love and touch as many people as you can. Stop hesitating, ruminating, or cogitating. Forget the excuses and rationalizations. They are all lies. Choose either to live or die. It's up to you.

Love Will Protect You

Allow yourself to become totally vulnerable. Only when you are willing to be totally vulnerable are you totally potent. When you are totally potent, others who would intimidate and victimize you will fall by the wayside. Let go of being afraid. Fear is their only weapon.

When you truly give up fear, people will respond to you with love. Your own children want to be with you, to touch, support, nurture, and love you. Unless you are open and vulnerable, they don't know who or where to find you. It is impossible to pass through a locked door. You have to make yourself known, and you have to open the door. It is up to you to let them know that you are alive and willing to live and love.

Advertise, if necessary. This is a wonderful way to reach people. Businesses do it all the time. I have received hundreds of thank-you letters from men and women who have found others through ads placed in personal columns.

Begin to talk with everyone, everywhere. Converse with people in supermarkets, elevators, restaurants, buses, planes, trains, and bathrooms. Don't negatively fantasize—communicate.

A short while ago, while taking a trip from San Francisco to Oakland on the Bay Area Rapid Transit (BART), a 25- or 30-year-old woman sat facing me. I struck up a conversation with her, as I almost always do, and asked her what she thought of BART. She hesitated for a moment (sizing me up, I guess) then said she hated going through the tube under the Bay. She was deathly afraid the tunnel would one day collapse and she would die a horrible death. She always felt claustrophobic in the tube. I proceeded to share some of my insights into fear and death. We talked about how she had lived so much of her life in fear. In 15 to 20 minutes, we became "friendly lovers."

She grasped my hands, told me how grateful she was for our conversation, and gave me a big hug and kiss. As the train approached her station, she asked me to join her for coffee and continue our conversation. The offer was attractive, but I declined. I told her that brief moment in time was priceless for me and I loved her for risking, first by talking with me, then by hugging and kissing me, and then by asking me to join her.

She had indeed made herself totally vulnerable. In that extremely short period of time, she overcame her fears. She stopped dying and started to live and love. Neither of us knew the other's name, but that didn't matter. We had a complete intimate relationship. We had both lived, laughed, touched, and loved.

I continually do this, and you can, too. Love other people: waiters, waitresses, clerks; people in department stores or on the street; everyone and anyone. Reach out and love. If you are alone and lonely, this is the perfect antidote. If you are scared of other people and wound in on yourself, this is the perfect unwinder. If you are married or in a relationship, it adds to those you love because you are interesting and loving. And if you are a parent, the joyous offering you give your children is better than the fanciest, costliest gift money can buy.

Begin now. You can create a truly loving world around you.

18

Our Future

To create a loving world is a huge undertaking. It may seem overwhelming. Don't let that stop you. As Margaret Mead said, *"Never doubt that a small group of thoughtful, committed citizens can change the world. Indeed, it's the only thing that ever has."*

Begin now by raising loving children and other people. Watch the ripples of love as they spread to others. For each person you touch touches others. Your personal realm can become increasingly more loving. Allow this love to spread to the far corners of the world.

Let love begin with you. I have started, and so have others. Now you can add the force of your love and commitment as well. We *can* live in a loving world.

How might this truly loving world look? Imagine yourself, your children, and the other important people in your life as partners. Imagine when you or any of them have a problem or a concern, all of you are there to support each other. Imagine you and your children dealing with each other openly and honestly about everything—no matter what. Even during those well-known teenage years, imagine you and your children working together, working things out with love.

Every little thing you do is a contribution. Begin now. Make a commitment to love. Your next thought, your next action, your next word can change the world.

W.H. Murray, in *The Scottish Himalayan Expedition,* has a wonderful insight into commitment:

> Until one is committed there is hesitancy, the chance to draw back, always ineffectiveness. Concerning all acts of initiative (and creation), there is one elementary truth, the ignorance of which kills countless ideas and splendid plans: that the moment one definitely commits oneself, then providence moves too.
>
> All sorts of things occur to help one that would never otherwise have occurred. A whole stream of events issues from the decision, raising in one's favor all manner of unforeseen incidents and meetings and material assistance, which no man could have dreamt would have come his way.

Use your commitment as a personal North Star, a place to head for, a goal. If you find yourself off course at times, don't be concerned. As with any navigational process, it is almost impossible to get directly from here to there. One cannot travel in a straight line. All such journeys, whether they be through land, sea, space, or personal growth, are a continual process of getting off course and correcting the course, veering, and compensating. Always true yourself back to your commitment—your North Star.

I have learned a deep respect for one of Goethe's couplets:

> Whatever you can do, or dream you can, begin it.
> Boldness has genius, power and magic in it.

The only thing to prevent your vision from becoming reality is your choice to believe it can't be done. The biggest danger is that at some point you may forget the principles of navigation. Being off course does not mean you are doomed to fail. It simply means you must change your direction and once again aim for your goal. It is your choice. What will it be?

If not you, who? If not now, when?

Acknowledgments

There are so many people who played important parts in getting this book written that it is virtually impossible to name them all. To those people I may have inadvertently omitted, I ask your compassion, understanding, and forgiveness. Any omission is definitely not intentional.

However, the architect of the humanity this book is built on is Helen Porter Dale, my wife of three and a half decades and the mother of our four sons. Although I have written this book in the first person, truly Helen with her guiding light and wisdom is behind every word.

Dan, Rex, Mark, and Scott Dale...four of the most tender, gentle, beautiful, intelligent, and loving sons any parent would be proud of. You did a wonderful job of raising me, guys.

Marsha and Mona...two beautiful daughters of a marriage that taught me more than I had ever bargained for. What intelligence, compassionate, and loving women they have become.

Janet Dale...for supporting me with pure, unconditional love for the past fifteen years. You are a beacon of pure love!

Jenise Dormann, without whose efforts this book would not be in your hands now, and her loving husband Aribert. Both are messengers of love and devotion.

Sonika Tinker and Debra Rein have added their editing skills, wisdom, and consciousness to this book and our workshops.

Joyce Patterson-Rogers for lending me her typewriter and a room in her home after a three-month sabbatical in the Mojave Desert, where this book was first conceived.

Floyd Goff, who is a valued spiritual teacher, friend, and facilitator. Thanks, also, to Griselda Tello, Robin Yarbrough, Peachey Roberts, Ed Tucker, Michael Hagerty, and Robin Taylor for being willing to serve whenever called upon. Also to Ann Hauser for editing and typesetting.

To Anne Watts, Peter Rengel, Chip August, Tedde Rinker-Jacobs, and Donna Spitzer, facilitators of the Human Awareness Institute workshops helping "Create A World Where Everyone Wins."

To all past, present, and future HAI Interns, and last but not least, Ken Keyes Jr., for having the vision, along with me, that love is the only answer. Ken is the true prophet of love for our time.

Human Awareness Institute
Workshops, Classes, and Events

Stan Dale is the founder of the Human Awareness Institute (HAI). It is HAI's mission to empower individuals to know the truth about who they are as potent, loving, contributing human beings. HAI is devoted to promoting personal growth and social evolution by replacing ignorance and fear with awareness and love. The Human Awareness Institute aims to create a world where people live together in dignity, respect, understanding, trust, kindness, honesty, and love.

The Human Awareness Institute is committed to creating a world where everyone wins. In support of this mission, the Human Awareness Institute offers a wide variety of workshops, classes, and events. These include six levels of the weekend-long Sex, Love & Intimacy Workshops; a One-Day Sex, Love & Intimacy Workshop; day-long workshops on Healing Anger, Heart Meditation, Opening to Sexual Intimacy; workshops for businesses on Team Transformations; as well as support groups, parties, meetings, and much more. HAI is based in Northern California and offers activities there, as well as around the U.S. and internationally.

Originating in Chicago, in the late 1960s, the Sex, Love & Intimacy Workshops have empowered approximately 30,000 participants to:

- Examine and shed limiting notions about sex, love, and intimacy;
- Relate and communicate more effectively with others;
- Significantly improve their relationships with themselves;

- Be more loving, intimate, and fully self-expressive;
- Make exciting and empowering choices in their lives and relationships that they never before thought possible.

These weekend workshops provide you with an opportunity to unleash your infinite capacity to love and be loved. You are supported in discovering and shedding the fears, judgments, and disempowering beliefs and behaviors that keep you separate from others. You are encouraged to explore new ways of relating and communicating that profoundly deepen your ability to be intimate.

Throughout the workshops you significantly improve your relationship with yourself. You uncover your beauty, power, and love for self through the simple magic of honesty and authenticity. This increased self-esteem, along with new possibilities for relating, allow you to make exciting and empowering choices in your life and relationships that you never before thought possible. Regardless of your relationship status or sexual preference, the Sex, Love & Intimacy Workshops are for you.

To allow more people to participate in this experience, HAI has created a special One-Day Workshop. This workshop is filled with direct experiences of love. You are given an opportunity to uncover your patterns of avoiding intimacy. In a caring, supportive environment, any walls around your heart gently melt. You discover the freedom of letting yourself love and be loved at levels you have always known were possible. And you go home with useful ways of allowing yourself to experience deeper intimacy. Whether you are single,

158

married, or in a relationship, regardless of your sexual preference, this day could be a turning point in your life.

For more information about these workshops, or any HAI activities, please call or write to:

Human Awareness Institute
1720 South Amphlett Boulevard,
Suite 128
San Mateo, California 94402
(415) 571-5524
1 (800) 800-4117

Also by Stan Dale:
Fantasies Can Set You Free

The dictionary defines fantasy as "creating mental images." It's what our minds do, all the time. Without realizing it, we allow our lives to be ruled by our fantasies. Our negative fantasies—particularly fear—are at the core of our problems. In *Fantasies Can Set You Free,* Stan Dale explores the awesome power of our fantasies, showing us how we can replace our negative fanta-

sies with positive ones that can transform our lives.

Fantasies Can Set You Free is also available on audio cassette. Narrated by Stan Dale personally, these tapes contain the complete text of the book. Learn about the awesome power of our fantasies as you drive your car or work around your house. Or give yourself a Stan Dale intensive, reading the book while simultaneously listening to the tapes.

160

Ordering Information

Books

$5.00   *Fantasies Can Set You Free*
$8.95   *My Child, My Self: How to Raise the Child*
          You Always Wanted to Be

Audio Cassettes

$25.00   *Fantasies Can Set You Free* (3 tapes)

Qty.	Item	Price	Amount
California Residents only: Pleae add applicable state sales tax.			
Prices include shipping and handling. **TOTAL**			

☐ **Yes!** Please put me on your mailing list and send me a free catalog listing workshops, books, posters, and audio and video tapes.

Ship to (please print) _____

Address _____

City _____

State _____ Zip _____

Telephone No. ( )_____

For ( ) VISA or ( ) MasterCard orders:

Card # _____

Exp. Date _____ Signature _____

Stan Dale's books may be obtained by mail order. Send your check in U.S. funds or credit card information to:

Human Awareness Institute
1720 South Amphlett Boulevard, Suite 128
San Mateo, California 94402

To order by phone with VISA or MasterCard call: (415) 571-5524 or 1 (800) 800-4117, Monday through Friday, 9:00 a.m. to 5:00 p.m. Pacific time.